PRAISE FOR *KILL BILLS!*

'It's a simple, no-nonsense book that will help anyone, even those who admit to having little financial nous. There's no doubt by the end of this book significant savings can be made that will hopefully help households have a little extra money in their pockets as they start the new year.' **Sophie Elsworth, *The Herald Sun* and *The Daily Telegraph***

'This is the perfect gift – it's like giving your friends a big wad of cash!!!' **Hamish, Booktopia review**

'The method of getting your bills down is essentially the same for each type of bill, but it was at least motivational enough for me to make some enquiries. Funnily enough, we spent 30 mins on the phone after reading the section on energy and gas bills, and would have saved about $1000 just like the cover said! I would recommend this book for all Aussie households.' **Em, Goodreads review**

'This book is so easy to read and understand. The best part is that you don't need to read it in any particular order – once you learn the lingo (which is quickly covered in the front portion of the book), you can flick between any chapter to tackle the bill you need to address. Once you get through this book, you will wonder why you didn't review your household bills sooner! The book has already paid for itself in tackling my first bill – money well spent!' **Tanya, Amazon review**

'Best audiobook I have ever downloaded and I'm only three chapters in! ... I am in the process of going through my home, contents and car insurance using the tips in the book and so far my annual cost of all three has gone from $3824 to $2087 ... that's an extra $243 per month back in our pockets! You HAVE to read this book!' **Kellie Owen, Facebook review**

EASY MONEY

7 STEPS TO BUST YOUR BILLS

JOEL GIBSON

London · New York · Sydney · Toronto · New Delhi

EASY MONEY: 7 steps to bust your bills
First published in Australia in 2023 by
Simon & Schuster (Australia) Pty Limited
Suite 19A, Level 1, Building C, 450 Miller Street, Cammeray, NSW 2062

10 9 8 7 6 5 4 3 2 1

Sydney New York London Toronto New Delhi
Visit our website at www.simonandschuster.com.au

A catalogue record for this book is available from the National Library of Australia

ISBN: 9781761109799

Cover design by Meng Koach
Internal illustrations by Rocco Fazzari
Author photograph supplied by RevTech Media
Typeset by Midland Typesetters, Australia
Printed and bound in Australia by Griffin Press

CONTENTS

PART 1 – THE 7 SIMPLE STEPS THAT COULD SLASH YOUR HOUSEHOLD COSTS

PART 2 – THE INSIDER TRICKS YOU NEED TO WIN THE WAR ON HOUSEHOLD BILLS

PART 3 – A BILL-BY-BILL BREAKDOWN (AND WHERE TO FIND THE EASY MONEY)

'Show me the money!'
Jerry Maguire

This book outlines an expanded and simplified version of the money-saving system I first described in my 2019 book *KILL BILLS!*

It's designed to help you fight the hip pocket impacts of the COVID-19 pandemic and the biggest cost of living crisis in a generation.

It also contains all you need to become a bona fide money-saving nerd without breaking a sweat and save thousands of dollars over time, but to state the bleeding obvious . . . it's a book, not a financial advisor! So it can't give you personalised financial advice.

Any advice contained in this book is general in nature and doesn't take into account your particular objectives, personal circumstances or needs. If in doubt about your own situation you should seek appropriate advice.

Also, I've done my best to make sure all the information is up to date at the time of publication, but things do change quickly. So, where possible, I've also given you a website or other place where you can check the latest information at the time of reading.

One Big Switch is a registered business name of RevTech Media Pty Ltd (ABN 75 150 963 474), holder of an Australian Financial Services Licence (AFSL 455982) and an Australian Credit Licence (ACL 405918).

PART 1

THE 7 SIMPLE STEPS THAT COULD SLASH YOUR HOUSEHOLD COSTS

CHAPTER 1
WHY I WROTE THIS BOOK (AND WHY YOU SHOULD READ AT LEAST SOME OF IT)

Like most people, there are about 457 things I'd rather do than think about money. Money can be a wonderful means to an end, but it can also be a major pain in the arse. So my goals for this book are as simple as the money-saving system I've outlined in it:

1. I want it to be the LEAST boring book about bills you've ever read;
2. I want it to save you thousands of dollars as EASILY as possible; and
3. I want it to make you feel GOOD about money.

Most of us are giving away hundreds or even thousands of dollars a year to businesses and governments that don't need or deserve it.

If we can get some of that money back, with minimal effort, it could be the easiest $1000+ we've ever earnt.

In 2019, I wrote *KILL BILLS!* to try and show everyone just how much power you have over your bills if you know how to harness it. With a bit of inside info and a few killer moves, anyone really can become a money-saving Ninja.

I know this because I was pretty hopeless with money until it became my day job. Like a lot of thirty-somethings, I was in debt and living payday to payday. But over the past decade, working at Australia's largest cost of living movement One Big Switch, as well as dishing out money-saving advice at *The Sydney Morning Herald*, *The Age*, the *Today* show and the ABC, I've gathered an armoury of tricks, hacks and loopholes that can save a household big bucks.

And it's never been more important to share them. Australians have just survived a once-in-a-century pandemic and we're now living through the toughest cost of living crisis in a generation.

As I write this, petrol prices are at record highs, power bills are rising by around $300–$400 a year, people have been known to pay up to $12 for a lettuce, rents are soaring and the average mortgage cost has risen by over $8,000 in the space of just six months.

I used to be that boring guy who talked about bills at barbeques. But bills aren't boring anymore – they're bloody terrifying. Now, people come up to me at barbeques and ask what they can do to get things under control.

So I knew I had to reinvent my system for slashing your household costs. I had to update it for a post-COVID world where everything is much more expensive. I had to make it better and I also needed to make it even simpler – to maximise your bang for buck.

You just want to know the easiest way to put hundreds or thousands of dollars back in your pocket with as little effort and time as possible. I get that. So I've reinvented the money-saving system in this book for 2023 and renamed it *Easy Money* – because that's what it's all about.

I won't claim this book makes bills fun. (I may be boring but not even I think bills are fun!) But if I've done my job, it will make bills a buzz – not the buzz you get from sipping a margarita or dancing or surfing or bungee jumping (or however you get your kicks), but if you've ever walked out of the gym or off the stage or returned home from a walk or a run or a swim with your endorphins pumping, feeling energized and about a metre taller, then you know the feeling. That's the feeling you'll get when you're winning at bills.

WHAT'S NEW IN THIS BOOK:

This 2023 update contains every money-saving trick, hack and loophole I revealed in *KILL BILLS!*, plus:

- How to save hundreds on streaming and pay TV costs;
- How to see if some of the BILLIONS of dollars of free money held by governments and banks belongs to you or your family;
- Crucial updates on the EASIEST ways to save on energy, telco, insurance and housing costs;
- NEW money-saving hacks for groceries and petrol; and
- More pictures of my dog, because there's no such thing as too many pictures of Sunny the Money-Saving Dog.

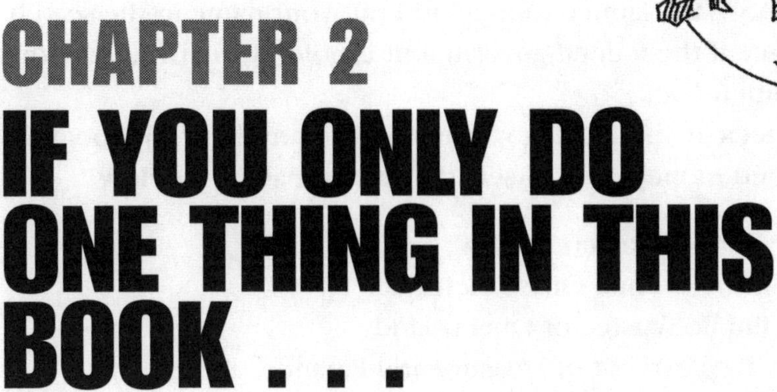

CHAPTER 2
IF YOU ONLY DO ONE THING IN THIS BOOK . . .

> 'The easy way is also the right way.'
> **Bruce Lee**

If you haven't got the time or energy to read the rest of this book, but you just really need to save some money, follow the 7 steps below and I'll be a monkey's uncle if you can't save a buck – or even $1000+.

A handful of common bills, a quick search for FREE money, a few hours of your time (at most), and $1000+ in potential easy savings. I call it the '7 Simple Steps of Money-Savers Anonymous'.

So make yourself a coffee or a tea (no beer or wine yet – save that for the after-party) and start the clock. Here goes nothing . . .

STEP 1: FREE MONEY

Typical result if you haven't done this before: $0–$1000. There's no guaranteed money here but if there is, it'll be the easiest money you ever earned.

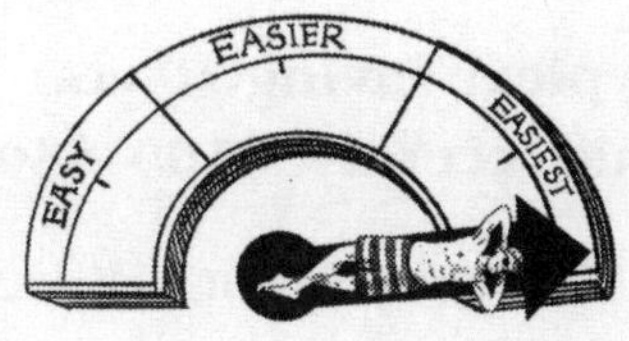

There's no easier money than free money, so let's start with a quick check to see if any of the BILLIONS of dollars in unclaimed money that Australian governments have sitting in their coffers belongs to you. It's a longshot, but I've seen people hit paydirt and it only takes two minutes.

- Google 'ASIC unclaimed money' and put your name in the search field to see if the federal government is holding anything for you. If so, claim it back.
- Next, check if the state government has anything by googling 'unclaimed money' and '[insert the relevant agency below]':

  If you're in NSW: Revenue NSW
  In VIC: State Revenue Office Victoria
  In QLD: Public Trustee of Queensland
  In SA: SA Department of Treasury and Finance
  In WA: WA Department of Treasury
  In the ACT: Public Trustee and Guardian for the ACT
  In the NT: Northern Territory Treasury
  In TAS: Tasmanian Department of Treasury and Finance, or phone (03) 6166 4188

Finally, if you've had homes in multiple states, it might be worth having a quick squiz at the other places where you've previously lived.

PRO TIP

You can also do these searches for friends and family, so pop their names in while you're at it.

STEP 2: FEEL THE POWER

Typical saving if you haven't done this recently: $100–$300.

- Next, grab your last electricity bill. Go to the government website EnergyMadeEasy.gov.au (or Compare.energy.vic.gov.au if you live in Victoria). Enter your details or just upload a PDF of your bill if you have one and the site will read your details for you.

- They will show you a list of deals ranked from cheapest to most expensive. Click 'Price with discounts' in the top right corner to see the discounts included in the prices. Now pick the plan you like the look of most out of the top three. (Note: this only works in South-east Qld, NSW, Vic, ACT, Tasmania and SA where switching is possible.)
- Next, go to OneBigSwitch.com.au (where I work) and see what the current group-discounted deal is in your state. (Reason: these don't always show up on the government website because they're not available to the general public.)
- You've now got two super-cheap offers in your hand. At this point, you can pick a winner and switch in under 5 minutes by filling out the online form – or you can call your provider (if you're fond of them) and ask them to beat what you've found. Here's your basic script:

'Hi there, my name is [Your Name Here]. I've been a loyal customer of yours for _______ years and I'd like to stay on, but I've just received two really good offers from other providers and I think they might be better than the one I'm on. _______ has offered me _______ and _______ has offered me ______. I wondered whether you can beat them? If you can, I'll lock it in right now. Perhaps you could put me through to someone on your Retention Team to see if they can help?'

You'll be amazed by how easy it is to switch your electricity provider – that's why around 2 million households do it every year.

STEP 3: YOU'VE GOT GAS?

- If you've got a gas bill, repeat the process above for natural gas and you can also save typically \$50–\$200 a year. If your new electricity retailer offered you a killer 'dual fuel' deal, go for it. But it's also just fine to have them both with different providers – and often cheaper.

- If you're in WA, use the website Wattever.com.au to compare current gas deals as they're not on the government sites I've listed above.
- Solar customer? It's a little trickier for you to pick a plan because it depends what sort of solar household you are – do you use most of your solar power or do you sell most of it back to the grid? Wattever.com.au is also a good site for comparing solar plans. Flick to the 'Energy' chapter later in the book for more detail.

STEP 4: TELCO TIME

Typical saving if you haven't done this recently: $100–$200 a year on mobile and $200–$300 a year on broadband.

Two bills down. Eat a biscuit. Blood sugar is important. Now let's see if your mobile deal is up to scratch. This will only take a few minutes.

- First, check your current plan so you know what you're comparing to: What do you pay each month? How much data do you get? What else is included? (Calls? Handset? International minutes? 5G network access?) Which mobile network is it on? Are you off-contract?
- Next, go to WhistleOut.com.au. Enter your info – data limits, inclusions and network (if you want a particular network for some reason – but otherwise select 'any'). They'll show you some options. (NB: They might show a couple of 'featured' ones first who pay for the top spot, but then they'll rank the rest from cheapest to most expensive.)
- Look at the cheapest 3–5 options and pick one that you like the look of most. Don't worry too much about making the perfect decision: they're all selling pretty much the same thing and you can take your number with you!

- If you're happy to switch, you can just sign up to the plan you've picked in minutes online. But if you really like your current provider, call them up and ask them to beat it. (Guess what? The script to use is the same as the one for energy bills above.)
- On a roll? Repeat the process above for your internet plan if you're not currently on a lock-in contract.

STEP 5: PLASTIC AIN'T FANTASTIC

Typical saving: $300 a year. More if you never use it again!

Eat an apple if you're feeling guilty about that biscuit you ate earlier. Now let's do something about your credit card (if you have one). Credit cards are the hidden household bill. The average balance is about $3000 and the average interest rate is almost 20% p.a. That can add up to about $600 a year. So, if you don't pay it off every month, we're going to switch to a zero-interest balance transfer card and pay it off, or at least switch to a low rate card and save hundreds on interest. Here's how:

- Go to Finder.com.au and click on 'Balance Transfer Cards'. You can sometimes pay no interest on the balance you move across for up to three years! Ideally, pick one that also has a low or no annual fee and a low or no 'balance transfer fee'.
- Pick a winning card from the top three and apply for it, then transfer your balance, move any direct debits you have set up onto your new balance transfer card, cancel the old credit card and chop it up.

PRO TIP

Leave the new balance transfer card encased in ice in the freezer and try not to use it. Ever. We're just using it as an interest-free tool to pay down your debt over a three-year period.

Take a quick break. Pat the dog. Stroke the cat. Think about what you're going to spend all your extra money on. Smile.

STEP 6: TIME TO STEP IT UP A LITTLE

Typical saving: $100–$400 a year.

That's the easiest of the easy money done. Now let's see what you can save on car insurance. Grab your last renewal so you have all the details of the policy. We're going to tackle this one a little differently.

- Go to your own insurer's website. Get an online quote using most of the same details as your current policy but change just enough to make yourself unrecognisable, Groucho Marx-style (you might have to use your neighbour's address as they will probably have yours saved). You now know whether they're charging new customers less than they're charging you for essentially the same policy.
- Next, go to one of the 'challenger brand' websites such as Budget Direct, Youi or Woolworths Insurance (up to you which one – they're all generally pretty cheap). Get a quick quote using the same details as your renewal.
- Now decide: do you want to switch or give your insurer a chance to keep you? If you want to give them a chance, the script for this one is similar but with a twist. All together now . . .

> *'Hi, my name's [Your Name Here] and I've been a loyal customer of yours for ______ years. I couldn't help noticing that you're charging me ______ more than you're charging a new customer with similar details to me. I know this because I got a quote on your website for a new policy with my details and I must have accidentally put my neighbour's address in. Whoops! Anyway, the quote came in at $_____. I've also got a quote from another insurer called _____ and it's only $_____. I'd like you to match or beat those other quotes, please, and if you can I'll renew right now. If you can't, I'm tempted to take my business elsewhere.'*

Use the same process above for your home or contents insurance and see if you can save about the same amount. Or ask the car insurer you've ended up with what they'll offer you to take out home insurance with them too. Sometimes they'll give you a multi-policy discount.

INSIDE INFO

Even if you've paid your insurance for the year, you're not locked in. You can always switch and ask for a refund of part of your premium, based on how many months are left in the year – that's what happens every time someone moves house, for example.

STEP 7: FEELING COCKY?

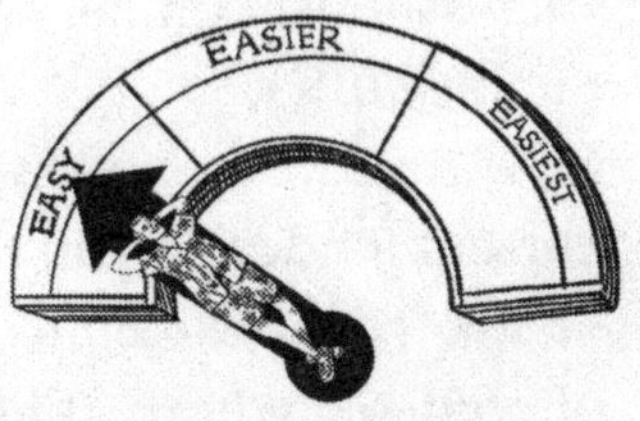

Typical saving: $500–$5000 a year. It all depends on how much your mortgage or rent is and how much you get the rate down.

Take a deep breath. You've already smashed up to six bills and hopefully put hundreds of dollars of easy cash back in your pocket where it belongs. This next one is another level entirely. Mortgage or rent payments are the Godzilla of household bills, so I'm not going to lie to you and say they're easy to take down. There are, however, smart ways and dumb ways to go about it. So if you're up for having a shot, let's start the process now. (If not, flick to the next section where I'll explain the theory behind why these money-saving tricks usually work.)

Still here? OK, mortgages first.

NUMBER CRUNCH

It costs a mortgage provider more than $1000 and often over $1500 in advertising and other costs for each new customer they attract. So if they're thinking straight, they should be prepared to give you hundreds in savings to stop you leaving.

- Check your current home loan interest rate. Even if you think you know it, it might have changed. It should be on a recent statement or in your internet banking profile.
- Don't want to speak to brokers? Go to Canstar.com.au or RateCity.com.au and check what the cheapest current interest rates are. Make a note.
- Happy to take calls from brokers? Ask friends for a recommendation or put your details in at an online mortgage marketplace such as Joust.com.au and you'll be contacted by the broker with the best offer.
- Now decide: do you want to switch or just negotiate with your current lender? If you're not ready to switch yet, call your lender or ask your broker to do so and tell them what you've been offered elsewhere. If you're armed with the above information, most times they'll play ball. If they don't, they probably don't deserve your business. You know the drill by now.

'Hi, my name is [Your Name Here] and I've been a customer for ______ years. I've just noticed my interest rate is ______% p.a. and there are now rates out there of ______% p.a. with ______ and ______% p.a. with ______. So I'm planning on switching. But I just thought I'd make one call to see if you can match it before I do. What's the best rate you can offer me to stay?'

PRO TIP

If you really want to play hardball, you can request a 'mortgage discharge form' which signals to the bank that you're getting ready to move.

Hello renters. You're probably sick and tired of being left out of the conversation, aren't you? The data says about one-third of us are renters, one-third are borrowers and one-third have paid off their mortgages. But you wouldn't know it. Renters are the forgotten people – like the fifth Beatle or the third member of Destiny's Child.

Anyhow, I haven't forgotten you! Real estate websites such as Domain.com.au and Realestate.com.au are your secret weapon here. You just need to follow the same process but look for similar rental properties advertised nearby or google recent listings to use as your leverage. Then, contact your agent and ask for a rent negotiation based on those real-world examples. As always, you've got to be prepared to walk if it comes to that. For inspiration, see this letter penned by my workmate Jess who did exactly that and saved $1500 a year on her rent.

Hi [Name of real estate agent],
Prior to renewing my lease I would like to discuss the possibility of a rent negotiation.

I have done some research online and saw that Unit 5 used images from my apartment and is leased for $495 per week, $55 less per week than what I pay.

Similarly, Unit 4, albeit not at the same standard as mine, is asking for $100 less per week than my apartment. It is however in the same location, the same size and with the exact same amenities.

I take excellent care of the apartment, pay my rent on time and I'm a respectable and considerate neighbour and tenant.

I believe a deduction of $30 per week is a fair and reasonable amount.

Could you please let me know if the landlord is willing to accept this offer.

Please also let me know if you would prefer to discuss this over the phone.

Kind regards,

Jessica

If these money-saving moves scored you some easy money, mission accomplished. You can close this book now if you want, but be sure to pick it up again in a year or so – even a killer deal can become a dud in 12 months.

On the other hand, if you want to know more about why this system works, or to become a full-blown money-saving nerd like me, then read on. We're just getting started . . .

CHAPTER 3
WHY THESE MONEY-SAVING TRICKS WORK

> 'Give someone a fish and they eat for a day. But teach them to fish and they eat for a lifetime.'
> **Centuries-old proverb, origin unknown**

Saving money is like fishing – you need some luck, but a bit of skill and insider knowledge goes a long way.

With the team at One Big Switch, Australia's million-member cost of living movement, I've spent the past decade trying to save Australian households money by negotiating with businesses on their behalf.

As a money-saving columnist and media commentator, I've also learnt a lot about how to gain an upper hand when dealing with the providers of your household bills.

The '7 Simple Steps of Money-Savers Anonymous' we just ran through are based on the best inside info, hacks and loopholes I've collected. If you just ran through those steps, you've used almost every one of the 'insider tricks' I'll outline in this book, even if you didn't realise you were doing it.

I give them names like 'The De Niro', 'The Elizabeth Taylor' and 'The Mystery Shopper' to help explain them in the next section.

So this book is a crash-course on 'fishing for savings'. I'll tell you what you should do to achieve the easy savings – the low-hanging fruit – and for the hardcore money-saving nerds I'll go into more detail on how you can really minimize what you spend on bills without sacrificing good service.

I'll give you even more simple scripts you can use to get a better deal from your provider, and I'll also look at some basic human traits that can stop us from being Bill-Killers if we're not aware of them – things like 'loss aversion', 'status quo bias', 'choice paralysis' and the big one: Aussies' mortal fear of haggling!

If it works for you, don't forget to tell the world about your wins. You'll inspire others to have a go and if we all talk about saving money more often, kids will grow up knowing more about it, businesses will find it harder to overcharge people, and I'll be a much more interesting dinner party guest.

HAD A WIN?

Brag about it! Tell a friend. Lend them this book or buy them one. And tag us in a post on Facebook, Twitter or Instagram at the following profiles:

Twitter: @joelgibson
Instagram: joelmgibson
Twitter: @OneBigSwitchAU
Instagram: OneBigSwitchAU
Facebook: OneBigSwitch

HOW I'VE SAVED MY FAMILY THOUSANDS OF DOLLARS USING THIS SIMPLE SYSTEM

One of the reasons I know these insider tricks work is that I've put my money where my mouth is and used them over and over again to save my family money in the past decade.

It didn't take me weeks of research and hours of wasted time on the phone to foreign call centres, because I knew the shortcuts to get a result.

In 2017, for example, our home loan interest rate had risen by about 90 basis points (0.90%).

Like thousands of Australians, it was because we had an 'interest-only' loan and regulators had been clamping down on them, causing banks to raise the rates on them. (The Australian Competition and Consumer Commission (ACCC) estimated they made an extra $1 billion in interest from people like me who didn't immediately refinance.)

I called our mortgage broker and said we were happy to move to a 'principal and interest' loan for a lower rate, and what could he negotiate for us?

So he called the bank and they offered a 0.60% reduction straight off the bat.

But we knew from experience that this was just their first offer.

I was also aware there were lenders out there offering variable rates with a '3' in front of them so I mentioned some of the examples I'd seen and asked him to keep pushing. 'If we have to move, we'll move,' I said.

So he went back to the bank and played hardball. In the end they knocked off 0.80% p.a. and we got a big bank rate starting with a '3'. We've got decades left paying off our home, so that should add up to a small fortune over time.

Saving: About $2000 p.a.

In 2018, tragedy struck: our wi-fi went down.

I busted the data cap on my mobile plan because we had no wi-fi at home. My kids nearly died of Netflix deprivation. We were all forced to read books! It was like the 1980s all over again.

I contacted our broadband provider and they said the local electricity network had replaced some poles and wires and accidentally cut the cable for our area.

For the next couple of weeks I hassled them for a date when it would be fixed, but they continued to blame the power company.

But then my wife told me she'd heard that if you lodge an official complaint with TIO (not your Spanish uncle, but in fact the

Telecommunications Industry Ombudsman), the provider has to open a file and allocate someone to resolve your issue.

So I did. Two weeks later, the internet came back on and the telco contacted me to wipe my excess data charges and offer a $459.80 bill credit for the internet (about seven months' worth).

A year later, we used the same trick to score my mum a $900 credit from her NBN provider!

Saving: Over $1400

True Story: How Mum got a $900 Telstra credit

My mum's NBN was super-slow, so I ran a test and found her download speed was only 2Mbps when it should have been 40Mbps.

She was getting nowhere with Telstra so I contacted my new best mate 'TIO' (remember him?) and even I was amazed by the result: within a week, Mum's NBN was fixed by NBN Co and Telstra did the right thing, offering her a $900 credit for months of lousy speeds!

In 2019, I chopped up my credit card.

Like most Australians, I'd had about $3000 of debt on a card for the past decade. Sometimes it was more, sometimes less, but like a yo-yo dieter, I always ended up back at about $3000 somehow.

Also like a lot of Australians, we had some savings sitting in another account, reducing the cost of our mortgage payments (an 'offset').

But this made no sense: I was paying 20% p.a. interest on my $3000 credit card debt while our savings were working to reduce the interest on my mortgage, where the rate was less than a quarter of that.

I decided to bite the bullet (once again, thanks to some encouragement from my wiser, better half), pay the card off and chop it up.

This has saved me as much as $600 a year in interest. Sure, I was getting points and it was handy to have, but being debt-free is better, and I've now got a debit card that I can use anywhere a credit card is welcome.

Saving: About $600 p.a. of 'money for nothing'

Like around half of Australians, I started my adult life as a Telstra customer.

When I got interested in money-saving, I switched to amaysim and got twice as much for the same price: 10GB of data for $40 a month. But the mobile market changes faster than just about any other household bill. As the data becomes cheaper for the providers, there's a sort of 'data creep' that occurs.

So a year later, I switched again when I saw Optus offering 30GB for $35. And about two years after that, I switched back to amaysim to get 55GB for $30, plus local and international calls.

I've never changed my number. My mobile plan now costs less than it did when I was 18 and contains about 20 times as much value.

Imagine if I'd stayed with Telstra all those years ...

Saving: Much more data for about $120 less p.a.

The energy industry has been one of the greatest exponents of the 'Honeymoon Strategy' pricing model: they often win you over with a very cheap one-year deal and then raise the price and hope to make money out of you in later years if you don't leave.

This happens because of two factors: annual price rises, and discounts that expire. In most states, tariffs usually go up each July. Meanwhile, after your 12-month discount ends, you usually get bumped to a lower discount, or none at all.

I can't say I've ever tested this one, but it's said that if you put a frog in a pot of boiling water it will leap out. However, put it in a pot of cold water and slowly heat it up, and you'll end up with a cooked frog (and probably a charge for animal cruelty – do *not* try this at home, it's just a metaphor).

The point of the boiling frog metaphor is that when things change gradually around us, sometimes we don't notice until it's too late.

And so it is with our power bills. Even a very good electricity deal can turn into an unhappy marriage over the course of a year, once the rates change and the discount expires.

Because of this, I've switched about ten times in eleven years.

2012: When I started working at One Big Switch, I'd never switched retailers before, so I moved our household to AGL because they had the best deal going at the time – a 17% discount.

2014: Two years later, we moved house and AGL moved us to a zero-discount plan. I questioned it and was moved onto an 'Under-the-Table' deal with a 24% discount.

2015: When my AGL deal expired, Origin was offering some of the best prices, plus over $100 in bill credits for switchers, so I moved again.

2017: Next up it was Red Energy, who was best-on-market in 2017 – so I moved both electricity and gas over.

2017: Something went wrong with the Red Energy switch because the meter reader couldn't get access to my meter, which was inside our front door. By the time I found out, the market had moved, so I switched to Powershop instead.

2018: A One Big Switch campaign unlocked a 30% electricity discount with Alinta, so I switched again.

2019: AGL called me again to offer 32% off electricity if I returned, so how could I say no?

2020: ReAmped, a new small retailer, was the cheapest provider in four states for most of 2020 and 2021 – so I thought I'd give them a try.

2021: ReAmped didn't do gas so I switched to a small Aussie retailer called Sumo for gas.

2022: When ReAmped imploded in the Great Energy Crisis of 2022, I noticed another small retailer called Nectr was offering a one-year fixed rate deal that was 20% less than the Government reference price, so I leapt at it. A day later, they closed the deal off.

Saving: Probably thousands.

So there it is – thousands of dollars worth of savings from just a few hours of haggling, complaining, switching and listening to my wife!

If someone offered you over $4000 for a few hours' work, wouldn't you take it? (You would. Even if it meant listening to your partner!)

To make the savings above, I used five of the insider tricks I'll outline in the next part of this book:

- the De Niro;
- the Elizabeth Taylor
- the Under-the-Table Deal;
- the Squeaky Wheel;
- the Moving Target; and
- the Good Listener.

Read on to understand how each of them works, how you can use them too, and a few others besides.

But first! Just in case you think you need to be an expert to get a result like this, below are the stories of some amateur 'super-switchers' who I've met in my travels and who achieved some of the biggest wins I've ever seen in the battle against household bills.

True Story: Leanne The Super-Switcher Saves $3749 In An Afternoon

Leanne from country NSW is a single mum with a high-powered job in IT. She's pictured here with me at the launch of *KILL BILLS!*

She's time-poor, but she put aside one afternoon and went on the equivalent of a money-saving lucky streak. Leanne killed five different household bills in that single afternoon and estimated afterwards that she saved:

- $610 a year on health insurance;
- $1595 a year on home and contents insurance;
- $777 a year on car insurance; and
- $333 a year on two mobile phones.

She also did a 'De Niro' on her energy provider (a move I'll explain in the next section), telling them she'd been offered a great discount elsewhere and was ready to walk. So they matched the offer she'd found, saving her an estimated $433 in the coming year on energy.

Add up the numbers and weep.

'I saved $3749, and it took me two hours to do it,' Leanne told *7 News*, who were so blown away by her results they did a story on her. 'I'm really tired of these vendors who take you for granted . . . I think we all need to just get more confident and switch!'

I asked her what her advice was to anyone who's ready to have a go.

'Just put aside the time, have the paperwork in front of you so you're prepared for the conversation and you're not fluffing around on the phone. Be confident but polite. Ask to speak to a manager. And I think it's best to focus on the big ticket items, particularly the annuity bills that come in every few months or every year like energy and insurance. But it is possible to save a lot of money, and sometimes you don't even need to switch to do it.'

True Story: Yvette, Bill-Killer Extraordinaire, Saves Over $6000 In 3–4 Hours

Yvette is a mother of four with a couple of Airbnb-style investment properties who learnt the art of the haggle working at her local fruit and veg markets.

After reading *KILL BILLS!*, she hit the phones and saved an amazing $6700 p.a. on a range of mortgages, insurance policies and energy plans. The breakdown of her savings was:

- Mortgages: $2448 p.a.
- Other loans: $900 p.a.
- Home Insurance: $1212 p.a.

- Car Insurance: $878 p.a.
- Life Insurance: $684 p.a.
- Cashback and credits: $280 p.a.
- Grocery discounts: $360 p.a.

Remember what I said earlier about the buzz you get when you have a big win and nail some easy money?

Well, don't just take it from me – Yvette was interviewed by the *Today Show* about her savings and she told them: 'It was the best 3–4 hours I think I've spent in a long time!'

PART 2
THE INSIDER TRICKS YOU NEED TO WIN THE WAR ON HOUSEHOLD BILLS

'Rule No. 1: Never lose money.
Rule No. 2: Never forget Rule No. 1.'
Warren Buffett

Here they are: nine insider tricks perfected by hardcore money-savers that I've come across in over a decade of helping people to save money on their bills.

They range from the 'De Niro' to the 'Mystery-Shopper', from the 'Elizabeth Taylor' to the 'Red Dog'. I've given them my own names but these bill-killing strategies are common knowledge to those who work in the energy, insurance or home loan industries - and unknown to many of us who don't.

If you've read *KILL BILLS!*, you'll already be familiar with these - I've made a few necessary updates but these are evergreen, perennial money-saving principles that won't change much over time.

Master them all, and the easy money will start to flow. Once they become habits, they can save you thousands of dollars over time.

CHAPTER 4
THE DE NIRO

This trick might just be the most important one of the lot.

I named it after one of my favourite movies – the 1995 Michael Mann gangster flick *Heat*.

In *Heat*, Robert De Niro plays Neil McCauley, a professional thief who never gets caught because – just like a shark – he never stops moving.

The movie gets its name from his most famous piece of advice:

> ‘*Don't let yourself get attached to anything you are not willing to walk out on in thirty seconds flat if you feel the heat around the corner.*’

(McCauley then falls in love, takes longer than 30 seconds to walk away from his girlfriend and ends up in a shootout with Al Pacino's cop character. For a long time, *Heat* was the only movie where they appeared in the same scene. I won't spoil the ending . . .)

But that De Niro attitude is what you'll need to channel if you're determined to pay as little as possible for your bills.

If you're not willing to walk away, if you're not ruthlessly and bloodlessly disloyal, you won't get the best deals or the easy money and sooner or later you'll end up being ripped off.

Many times you won't need to move at all. But just being prepared to switch providers will show you're serious about saving. It puts you in a completely different class of customer – a group that businesses call the ‘Price-Chasers’.

Businesses know they have to work that little bit harder to win over the Price-Chasers – so they often do.

True Stories: From Dickie Wilkins To Russell From Queensland, The 'De Niro' Is A Winner

When Channel Nine entertainment guru Richard 'Dickie' Wilkins told me he had a shocker of a power bill, I suggested I introduce him to the De Niro.

Dickie's probably met the real De Niro, but in this case I meant the money-saving trick, not the two-time Oscar winner.

So we called his power company and asked them to please explain why, as a longstanding loyal customer, Dickie was only receiving a 4% discount.

They offered to increase it to a 26% pay-on-time discount on the spot, but we explained that he'd been offered a massive 42% pay-on-time discount elsewhere.

So they put us through to the 'retention team', who increased the offer to a 28% guaranteed discount and a free smart meter (worth about $200), which was good enough to keep him – for now.

Fellow TV star Lisa Wilkinson also knows the value of the De Niro. On Channel Ten's *The Project*, she said she'd been looking at switching through a 'group-buying syndicate' until she got a call from her retailer at the last moment.

'[My electricity company] said, "We're going to give you a 15% discount!"'

But Lisa told them: "You know what? I'm still going to call that buying group." They called again and came back with an offer of 18%. In the end, I ended up with 28% discount, and all because I just kept saying no.'

Russell, a One Big Switch member from Queensland, isn't quite as famous as Richard or Lisa but he plays just as tough – and proves you don't need to be a big name to achieve a big result: 'Although I did not take up the offer [from One Big Switch] I used the offer to negotiate a better deal with my current supplier. I have done this on every occasion you have had an Energy Switch campaign. I also did this with the Health Insurance campaign. Just wanted to let you know that although I haven't taken up the winning offers, I still obtained better deals. Keep up the good work!'

Same to you, Russ!

The essence of the 'De Niro' is leverage. (As Lord Nelson once said, 'A fleet of British ships of war are the best negotiators in Europe.') So before you can threaten to leave, you've got to have leverage – and the best leverage is to have in your hot little hand a really good offer from another provider.

If your current provider can match it, you can choose to stay. If they can't or won't match it, you can switch.

Either way, you win.

Here's the basic De Niro script to use when you call your provider up – no matter which bill you're trying to reduce. It's up to you whether you read it in a 'you talkin' ta me?' New York taxi driver accent or not (but I'd advise not):

'Hi there, my name is [Robert De Niro/Richard Wilkins/Lisa Wilkinson/Russell from Queensland]. I've been a loyal customer of yours for _______ years and I'd like to stay on, but I've just received a really good offer from another provider and I think it might be a better deal than the one I'm on. _______ has offered me _______. I wondered whether

you can match it or even beat it? If you can, I'll lock it in right now. Perhaps you could put me through to someone on your retention team to see if they can help.'

Are you a 'Price-Chaser' or a 'Sleeping Beauty'?

Report after report has found that loyalty is all but dead when it comes to household bills. It's the customers they call 'Price-Chasers', those who are *most* prepared to move, who usually get the best deals. And too often it's the loyal, rusted-on customers who pay extra to help fund the deals for new customers.

Take power prices, for example. The ACCC spent a year looking into why our power prices are some of the highest in the world and concluded this:

> *Those customers who have been active in the market, regularly reviewing options and switching between offers … are likely paying less than the average cost to retailers of supplying electricity.*
>
> Source: ACCC © Commonwealth of Australia

(Translation: power companies were *losing* money on the customers who regularly moved plans or providers!)

There's a saying in some businesses that it doesn't pay 'to wake the Sleeping Beauty'.

The 'Sleeping Beauty' is a longstanding, loyal customer who never reads a book like this one, never asks for a better deal and never, ever leaves. The only way businesses can afford to cover the cost of attracting the 'Price-Chasers' above is to make extra margin out of these so-called 'Sleeping Beauties'.

This cross-subsidy is the backbone of whole industries, from energy to insurance and home loans. It's not fair but it's the way of the world.

The charity St Vincent de Paul, better known as Vinnies, takes an annual look at the difference between what Price-Chasers pay for electricity, by shopping around for the cheapest offers on the market, compared to Sleeping Beauties, who end up on the most expensive 'standing offers'.

In 2018, the gap reached as much as $2675 a year for two hypothetical Victorian households using the same amount of energy! These days, thanks to some government reforms, it's more like up to $500 difference. That's still a big 'Loyalty Tax' to pay just for doing nothing.

Insurance is often the same. Former consumer watchdog Allan Fels did some research that estimated the old, loyal Sleeping Beauty customers pay 34% more than the new Price-Chaser customers for home insurance.

So if you're a Sleeping Beauty, you need to understand that money is falling out of your pockets while you slumber and it's being swept up and used to give all the De Niros out there great deal after great deal (or steal after steal!).

CHAPTER 5
THE UNDER-THE-TABLE DEAL

Contrary to what a lot of consumer advocates tell you, most businesses aren't inherently bad. They're not trying to screw you at every possible opportunity.

Businesses are not immoral; if anything, they're 'amoral'. They're like machines or robots that are programmed to provide a service in exchange for money. They're motivated by profit, of course, but not by malice.

But the thing about a robot is this: if you know how the machine works, you can usually beat it at its own game.

I remember learning a vital lesson about prices as a kid. I grew up around the snowfields on the NSW/Victoria border and my childhood hero was my dad's best mate Walter: a big, Swiss mountain of a bloke.

Like a lot of our family friends, Walter worked at one of the ski resorts, and one day I asked him how they set the price of a lift ticket.

'They charge $50,' he explained in his matter-of-fact Swiss way, 'because if they charge $60, the mountain isn't full. And if they charge $40, it's too full.'

I was dumbfounded. I always assumed they set the price as low as they could, to compete with other resorts.

I thought their formula was:

Lift ticket = cost of providing service + small margin

But no – they charged *as much* as they could without driving too many people away. The equation was actually:

Lift ticket = cost of providing service +
maximum margin possible without empty mountain

As a grown-up, I can now see it makes perfect sense. Businesses will charge you what you're prepared to pay.

This drives people *crazy*. Why should we have to ask for their best deal? Why don't we get rewarded for loyalty? This is BS!

All of which is true. But look at it the other way around: here we are, trying to work out how to pay *them* as little as possible for their services and take back some of that easy money we've been overpaying. So we're playing the game too. And if you're reading this book, you're playing to win.

Most businesses have several offers:

1. Their Base Offer, for anyone silly enough to take it. This one makes them the most money, so they dangle it out there just in case.
2. Their On-Market Offer, for those who ask for something better, but don't push them all the way.
3. Their 'Under-the-Table' Offer, for those customers they really need to work hard to keep.

How do you get the Under-the-Table offers? Once again, the key is leverage, and there are a couple of ways to get yourself some of that.

You can threaten to leave, which often leads to your provider making you a so-called 'retention offer'.

Some big businesses have whole teams who *just* work on 'retention'. When they hear you're leaving, they will put you through to the 'retention team' or you'll get a barrage of calls from them. Pick up the phone! That's when you know you're about to be made an offer that's very, very hard to refuse.

But of course, it pays to have a Plan B before you make that threat. Otherwise they can call your bluff.

So first, use brokers, comparison sites and buying groups like One Big Switch to find an alternative offer that gives you leverage.

There's never been more help out there for consumers looking to save: whether it's businesses to help you or digital tools or competition.

True Story: My Mate Mutchy Got A 30% Discount, Just By Asking

I was having a few quiet beers with my mate Mutchy one night and I asked him what energy deal he was on. He said he was getting a 20% discount.

I'd heard from some of our members that his provider had been offering 30% under the table to try and keep some customers who planned to leave.

So we harnessed our Dutch courage and rang and told them we'd seen a 30% discount from another provider available via One Big Switch (also true), and they matched it on the spot.

All up, it took about five minutes on the phone and saved him a couple of hundred dollars a year.

So I made him pay for the beers.

CONSUMER PSYCHOLOGY 101: Why westerners are lousy hagglers

It's not you. It's us. It's a cultural thing. Many Australians just find haggling difficult.

The travel Bible *Lonely Planet* tells foreign visitors that 'haggling isn't part of Australia's commercial culture', so don't bother.

According to a 2017 survey of 1700 people around the world, Aussies placed ninth out of 16 countries for 'enjoying' a haggle, and a lowly 15th out of 16 for the results we get - partly because our shops and service providers don't often encourage it.

A 2016 survey by Mozo found that we are most likely to haggle on whitegoods, but only 60% of us have tried it - saving an average of $139. In 2021, a Finder survey found two thirds of us don't haggle when buying a car and around a quarter of us aren't comfortable haggling at all.

These days we do haggle a bit for cars, for furniture and whitegoods and that sort of thing, because we've become used to The Good Guys, Harvey Norman and Bing Lee encouraging it.

We might go back and forth a bit with someone on Facebook Marketplace or on Gumtree. 'Tell 'im he's dreaming!' But compared to somewhere like Asia, it's just not as ingrained in us.

In 2013, researchers surveyed over 200 Chinese and Australian negotiators about their haggling 'tricks' for the *Journal of Business Ethics*.

They ran them through the 36 classic tactics outlined in an ancient Chinese essay on strategy, called *The Secret Art of War: The 36 Stratagems*.

They found Aussies were more comfortable feigning negative feelings or emotions in a negotiation, or using threats to win!

But the Chinese were more comfortable with most of the stratagems – and therefore presumably more comfortable with using haggling and negotiating tricks in general.

This fits well with the impressions of Aussie travel writer Ben Groundwater, who believes there's a word for people like him who find haggling a real chore: they're called 'Westerners'!

> *'We're just not built for this game. You never have to haggle over anything in the Western world ... The shopping experience for us is a cut-and-dried game. There's a price: you either pay it or you don't.'*

So if the thought of asking your power or insurance company for a better deal makes you feel awkward, you're not Robinson Crusoe. You're quite typical.

But once you've tried it and had a win, once you know who to haggle with and what to say, I think you'll find that haggling is kind of addictive. Once you get a sense of the power you have as a customer – a power we all have but maybe don't realise or exercise fully – there really is no stopping you.

CHAPTER 6

THE MYSTERY-SHOPPER

When I was a uni student, my mate Cal called me to say he'd found the perfect uni job.

'All you have to do,' he said, in a state of gobsmacked disbelief, 'is go shopping! And then you just write a report on how lousy the staff were, and they pay you!'

They're called 'mystery-shoppers', and businesses use these under-cover agents to check up on their own employees and franchisees.

It's pretty dastardly. But real customers can use this one to gain an advantage over businesses, too. Here's how.

Most businesses put their prices up every year, to cover inflation and increases in their costs. But some businesses also put their prices up to make more money out of you, even if their costs haven't risen by that much – mainly because they think they can get away with it.

If you ran through the 7 Simple Steps at the start of the book, then you've already had some practice at exploiting this loophole. So let's go mystery-shopping!

How to do a Mystery-Shop

1. Put on some dark glasses and a fake moustache, Groucho Marx-style.
2. Go to your provider's website.

3. Enter the same details as your current deal or policy, e.g. '$500,000 of home and contents cover on a three-bedroom freestanding house, built in 1960', etc. (Tip: these details should be on your renewal notice if you need to check them.)
4. BUT WAIT! Don't use the same name or address. This is because they will probably have yours stored already. Instead, use a different name (such as your partner's) and a different address in the same postcode (such as your neighbour's, where the risk profile of the suburb should be identical).
5. See what price they quote you. If it's the same as your current price, you're on a winner! Renew your policy and spend the rest of the day at the beach.
6. But if it's radically lower than your own price, you've got every right to ask them to 'please explain'. When faced with your research, most businesses will negotiate to keep you – offering you sometimes hundreds of dollars in easy money. If they don't, maybe it's time to get a quote from another website . . .

Once again, here's a basic script to use when you've done a Mystery-Shop:

> *'Hi, my name's [Groucho Marx/Robert De Niro/Insert real name here] and I've been a loyal customer of yours for ______ years. I've recently received my renewal notice. I couldn't help noticing that it's gone up by _____. And I also couldn't help noticing that it's ______ more than you're charging a new customer with similar details to me. I know this because I got a quote on your website for a new policy with my details and I must have accidentally put my neighbour's address in. Whoops! Anyhow, the quote came in at _____. How is that fair? I'd like you to match that new customer price please, and if you can I'll renew right now. If you can't, I've got a quote from another provider and I'm tempted to take my business elsewhere.'*

If you don't get the result you're after at first, ask to speak to their manager! (More on that coming up in 'The Squeaky Wheel'.)

CONSUMER PSYCHOLOGY 101: What is 'anchoring'? And how can you use this classic marketing tactic to your own advantage?

Around 50 years ago, two Israeli psychologists identified a number of ingrained consumer habits in a series of experiments that ended up winning them the Nobel Prize.

Daniel Kahneman and Amos Tversky called these habits our 'systematic biases'. They went on to become known as the pioneers of behavioural economics, which now influences how businesses sell us stuff, how governments convince us to do stuff, and (from this point on) how you and I resist being manipulated by those businesses and governments.

One of the biases or habits they identified was called 'anchoring' and it's behind a lot of the marketing and political campaigning that's targeted at us every single day of our lives.

'How much would you expect to pay for this robot vacuum cleaner?' asks the guy in the late-night infomercial. '$2000? $1000? No! It's yours for just four easy instalments of $199.99!'

Why does he start with a question you've never really asked yourself, and then answer it for you before you've had a chance to think about it, like Kevin Rudd used to do?

Because he's dropping an 'anchor' for you with the higher prices, which he hopes will set your expectation. And then he's undercutting it with the real price, to make it seem cheap.

On price tags and stickers, you see it all the time. 'Recommended Retail Price: $35. Our Price: $25!'

Experienced negotiators use anchoring all the time too. They'll start with an 'ambit claim' or a borderline-outrageous request in a bid to anchor expectations. They hope this then gives them a better chance of achieving their real aim, which is less ambitious.

'My client deserves a $50,000 pay rise.'

'Your client can have $10,000.'

'How about $15,000?'

'Deal!'

Even charities do it. When they ask, 'How much would you like to donate? $50, $100 or $500?' they're 'anchoring' you to think that $50 is the norm, or the starting point, because research and experience shows the average donation will be higher this way than if they gave options starting at, say, $20.

Human beings need these anchors. They put the 'educated' in our 'educated guesses'. If someone doesn't give them to us, we find our own.

But knowledge is power, of course, and now that you understand how anchoring works, you too can enlist it to hunt down easy money in the war on bills. Here's how.

Anchoring is a vital element in employing the 'De Niro' or in accessing 'Under-the-Table' deals, for starters. As I said earlier, your best chance of getting one of these deals is when you've already got another good offer to use as leverage. That other offer is your 'anchor'.

When you tell your provider 'I've just been offered a 30% discount on my electricity' or 'I can get sports on Kayo for only $25 a month, so why would I keep paying over $100 for Foxtel?' you've just given *them* an anchor.

They now know where the psychological starting point is to try to win you over.

Anchoring is also vital in the 'Mystery-Shopper' trick I've just described. Your mystery-shopping expedition creates an alternative quote.

Even if it's not a 100% real quote (because you've used your neighbour's address details, for example), it becomes a very real anchor for your insurer.

It's one of *their* quotes, and that makes it pretty hard to argue against. So they will often try to match it or compromise with you if they can.

In most cases, the best way to find a good 'anchor' for your negotiation is to be internet-savvy, which we'll talk about later in the section 'David's Slingshot'.

CHAPTER 7
THE ELIZABETH TAYLOR

'Your energy plan will be renewed, Joel,' said the letter I received a few years back from my electricity provider.

But the fine print revealed they'd 'renewed' me on a discount 10% lower than I had the previous year. Ever received one of those letters?

This practice is rife, especially when it comes to power and insurance companies.

In business it's known as a 'front book versus back book pricing strategy', where your 'front book' is made up of those new customers who receive attractive joining offers (remember the 'Price-Chasers' from earlier?), while your 'back book' is full of all those 'Sleeping Beauties' on old prices or rising prices who kindly pay extra to help fund the newbies.

NUMBER CRUNCH

Research by the NSW Insurance Levy Monitor has found that some sophisticated companies employ teams of highly skilled actuaries to create algorithms that predict precisely how much they can increase your price before you'll leave them.

That same report found that existing customers who renew their home insurance pay on average 34% more than new customers.

Whatever you call it – 'back-booking', 'the loyalty tax', 'the lazy tax', or 'don't wake the Sleeping Beauties' – entire industries have been built on this pricing model.

From a customer's point of view it looks like this:

1. First, they give you a very cheap one-year offer to win you over (sometimes they're even prepared to lose money on you in the first year if that's what it takes).
2. Then, they quietly wind back your discount, or increase your rate or premium. And because of our human traits of 'status quo bias' and 'loss aversion' (which I'll explain later), they take a punt that you'll be too busy or too lazy or too afraid of change to dump them.
3. Finally, they make their money out of you in years two, three and four – provided your natural aversion to change still proves strong enough to stop you from switching or complaining.

Companies do this because it works: extensive testing and experience have shown it time and time again. Most of us don't want to shop around or move providers every year. Who has the time and energy for that, right?!

But that's the insider trick here: this kind of 'Honeymoon Strategy' employed by businesses actually creates another easy money loophole to exploit. If you're prepared to move regularly, you can win and win again from this business model.

You can see where I'm going here. The way to pay as little as possible for your power bills and a range of other bills too is to adopt the 'Elizabeth Taylor' approach and take honeymoon after honeymoon after honeymoon.

You can honeymoon with different providers and sometimes even with the same provider more than once (hello again, Richard Burton!).

And sometimes you don't even have to leave to get a second honeymoon – when your plan goes up in the second year and you call the provider and say 'WTF', they will often bring it back down and give you another Price-Chaser deal to stay.

So don't end up in an unhappy marriage with your providers. There are plenty of other fish in the sea. Switch or negotiate a better offer if you see your price rise suddenly. And don't be afraid to do it again and again for energy, telco and insurance products (but not for credit products – too many applications for credit products can damage your credit rating).

The gap between the honeymooners and the Sleeping Beauties can be either a pitfall or an opportunity. It's up to you.

True Story: Glenn* Switches Health Insurance Again And Again, And Saves Up To 60%

Glenn (not his real name) is the Liz Taylor of Australian health insurance. He switches repeatedly – sometimes multiple times a year – to cash in on the deals for new members.

'It sometimes saves me up to 60% per annum,' he confided in me. 'It's so simple to change providers – I move on the day after each offer ends.'

Because of the laws around community rating in Australia, health funds cannot deny anyone cover. Also, if you've served a waiting period with another fund and you switch to similar level cover, you don't have to serve the waiting period again – it's 'portable'.

'Each time I switch I just send my clearance certificates to the new fund and get six weeks free or hundreds of dollars cashback,' Glenn said. 'What can they do about it? Nothing. Their only options would be to increase the eligibility period or decrease the promotional value – but because most people can't be bothered, I guess they just have to wear the cost of people like me.'

More power to you, I say! That's the sort of ingenuity we need when there's a cost of living crisis.

CHAPTER 8
THE MOVING TARGET

Do you know what the hardest thing is about winning the war on bills? Bills don't stand still!

You can switch your electricity plan but the following July the rates increase by hundreds of dollars and suddenly you're not on the best plan anymore.

You can sign up for a killer home loan rate but then your bank raises it by a hundred basis points, or you find a great insurance offer that saves you a packet but come your next renewal, your premium jumps by 20%.

Each bill is a moving target and you can win battle after battle but the war is never really over.

But here's the thing: the 'Moving Target' creates another opportunity for you to save some easy money.

Why? Because each time the market changes, there's a chance you can get a better deal for your dosh than you had before.

The key here is to identify markets where prices are *dropping*. These are rare in this day and age, but in those examples, you'll find you get better and better bang for the same buck by moving plans regularly.

Set and forget, on the other hand, and you'll end up marooned on an old pricing tier when the tide goes out – like that feeling when you buy a new TV and you see a bigger, better model at a lower price a month later.

The best examples of household bills where prices are *dropping* and inclusions are growing are mobile and broadband – because the technology is moving so fast.

Consider this: it used to be common for people to pay $100 a month for mobile or broadband plans with not much data.

Now, it's common to see plans for $60 a month with unlimited data (for broadband) or about $30 a month for 50GB of data (for mobile – that's enough to watch about sixty episodes of *Stranger Things* or *Game of Thrones*).

This is happening for two reasons: one, we are using so much more data every year, and two, the cost of data is dropping for the providers.

In late 2022, for example, Aussies downloaded 9.7 million terabytes in a three-month period. In 2011, we only downloaded about 274,000 terabytes (less than 3% of that amount) over the same time period!

So we're now downloading or streaming more than thirty-three times as much data as eleven years ago!

But in 2011, did an internet plan or a mobile plan cost any less than it does today? Not really. NBN plans now cost about $60–$100 a month, which was roughly what we paid for dial-up internet in the early days.

The graph below from the Australian Bureau of Statistics is one of those pictures that's worth a thousand words. It shows how our downloads have skyrocketed.

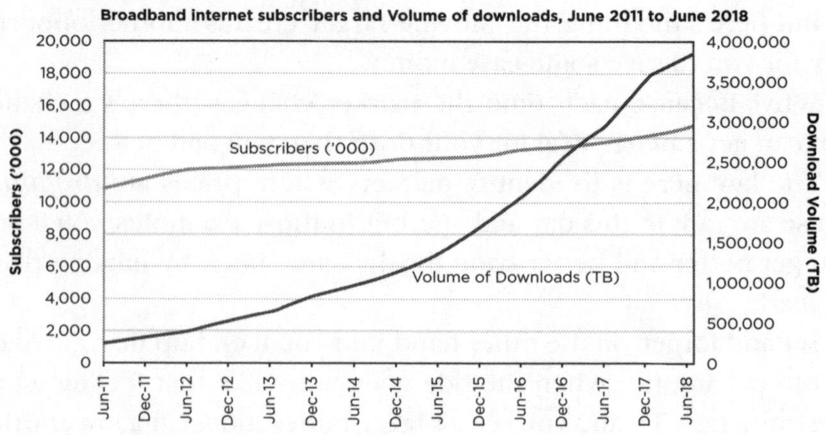

Source: Australian Bureau of Statistics

This target moves very quickly and you have to ride the rocket!

True Story: How Some Telcos Have Learnt A Thing Or Two From The Hare Krishnas

My first ever ADSL broadband plan had a 300GB download limit. Not long after I signed up, the provider (iiNet) contacted me to say they'd upgraded us to a 1000GB download limit.

I nearly fell out of my chair. There must be some mistake, I thought. Who gives anyone anything for free these days, apart from the Hare Krishnas?

Hello Joel

We've made our list and checked it twice, and you're definitely on it. To celebrate the festive season, we've got a nice upgrade for your current broadband plan to give you an extra helping of quota every month! That's right - it's not just for Christmas; you'll get your new quota every month from now on.

Naked Home - 1
$69.95 /month

Old Quota : 300GB

But my telco had in fact borrowed an age-old trick pioneered by that brightly robed, shaven-haired, chanting crew from the International Society for Krishna Consciousness.

The Hare Krishnas have long had a successful fundraising technique that involves giving out flowers and then asking for a donation. Most people take the gift, and then find it hard to say no when asked for a few bucks.

This trick was so effective that the state of California ended up banning them from airports!

What's that got to do with my old telco? Well, they locked me in for years with that gift. They bought my loyalty. What I didn't realise at the time was that it cost them virtually nothing. The extra data was a gift of sorts (they didn't have to give it to us) but the data was costing them less and less each day so it cost them no more to give us more. And, of course, because we'd signed up for 300GB, we really didn't need 1000GB so we didn't use it all.

I thought this was a one-off thing but then, ten years later, I switched my mobile to amaysim and they Hare-Krishna'd me too!

I've since done some work for amaysim as their 'moneysaver-in-residence' and they told me they have their own name for this practice: they call it 'rainbowing'.

Moral of this story? Telcos should periodically give us more for the same price (and if they don't, we should change plans regularly).

Oh, and more businesses should 'rainbow' their customers! They might find we're more loyal if they show us some loyalty first.

CONSUMER PSYCHOLOGY 101: 'Satisficers' versus 'Maximisers'

At this point, I think it's important to let you off the hook.

In this book I want to demonstrate how to really show your bills who's boss, with minimal time and effort. What I *don't* want to do is make you feel guilty if you're not always on the absolute best option.

You don't *have* to switch every bill every year. You don't *always* have to get the best Under-the-Table deal. You don't have to move every time the telco market does. Who's got time for all that? Not me, nor you. Life is short, after all.

These are general principles and the important thing is that you know them and you do these things from time to time. But don't be too hard on yourself.

It's bizarre but sometimes being a perfectionist can lead to doing nothing at all.

American psychologist Barry Schwartz really hit this nail on the head in the noughties when he told people:

'"Good enough" is almost always good enough.'

In his bestselling book *The Paradox of Choice: Why More is Less*, Schwartz's research found you're actually more likely to be happy in life if you're what he called a 'satisficer'. 'Satisficers' are happy to settle for 'good enough'.

'Maximisers', on the other hand, who always have to find the absolute *best* or *cheapest* option, are less satisfied with their lives. (They do earn more, mind you, but they're also more likely to regret their decisions, and to be depressed.)

It used to be that there was only one government-owned energy or telco provider (there still is in some parts of Australia). A lot of us are very nostalgic for those days: why do we have to chase down a better energy or mobile deal? Why have we created all this work for ourselves?

Schwartz says we've created so many choices in our modern lives that it can confuse us and make us miserable. In one famous study, psychologists presented 24 different types of jam to shoppers and gave them a voucher for $1 off a jar. But they bought less jam than another group of shoppers who were presented with just six options.

'Unconstrained choice,' he says, 'is paralyzing, not liberating', and he has a point.

Let's say you need to choose a laptop from the thousands of options now available to us. His tip is:

> *Whenever you need a new laptop, call up one of your maximizer friends and say, "What laptop did you buy?" And you buy that laptop. Is it going to be the perfect laptop for you? Probably not. Is it going to be a good enough laptop for you? Absolutely. It takes you five minutes to make a decision instead of five weeks and it's a "good enough" decision.*
>
> *'I don't think you can delegate all of the decisions in life in this way but you can certainly delegate a hell of a lot of them. What's best for your friend won't be best for you but chances are it will be good enough for you.*

There's no need to be on top of every bill all the time. I'm certainly not.

Just don't let yourself do the opposite, which is nothing. The biggest mistake we can make when it comes to our bills is to do nothing at all. Hopefully this book will show how even a small effort can produce big savings.

Which brings us to the next trick you need to master: listening . . .

CHAPTER 9
THE GOOD LISTENER

This next trick's not rocket science, but there's plenty of science to say it works.

Sometimes, all you have to do to save hundreds or thousands of dollars of easy money is to ask around.

'Word of mouth' is the #1 most trusted source of information when we make purchasing decisions, according to the *Nielsen Global Trust in Advertising Survey*.

It's almost twice as trusted as what we read in the media:

- 92% of us trust recommendations from friends,
- 70% trust online reviews, and
- 58% trust editorials or articles.

The management consultants at McKinsey believe that word of mouth plays a role in up to 50% of all purchasing decisions, and is *twice* as powerful as paid advertising.

So the first thing we should do when we want to save on insurance or energy or our home loan is ask around.

It works: people close to you will feel like they own the result of their recommendations, so they're unlikely to tip you into a deal that's no good (unless they don't realise it yet).

And someone you know might actually be something of an expert on that particular bill – so tapping into your network is a no-brainer.

There are a few different ways that being a 'Good Listener' can save you big bucks over time.

Ask an expert

Obviously, if you know someone who works in the banking, energy or insurance industry, for example, or just has some inside knowledge, go there first.

As I hope this book shows, a bit of inside info can prove priceless.

Friends regularly ask me what the best energy offer is, for example. It changes every month, and it all depends on what you need, so the answer is never straightforward. But I love being able to help them out.

By the same token, when I want to know what the cheapest home loan is this week or the most generous savings account, I usually contact the experts at RateCity or Canstar.

The cheapest petrol? I'll check in with the team at EzySt and Ruckus Energy Co., who are always watching the price cycle. Your network is one of your greatest strengths.

These days, there are quite sophisticated comparison sites for most household bills too, so you can get a really quick sense of what's available (except for those Under-the-Table deals, of course).

Ask your 'friends'

Social media isn't just good for posting selfies and cat memes. It's also a great way to tap into the so-called 'hive mind' or the 'wisdom of the crowd'.

Ask a question like 'Where's the best coffee in Melbourne?' or 'Top ten albums of all time?' on Facebook and you'll almost break the internet.

But I've found you also get a great result when you ask for people's money-saving tips. We don't always post this stuff pro-actively, but we do tend to respond when someone else starts the conversation.

So why not use that collective wisdom to solve problems like 'What's a good broadband deal at the moment?' or 'Anyone got any tips for getting my power bill down?'.

We're all in this war on bills together and people love to work with each other to even the playing field with these large, sophisticated businesses that provide our power or insurance or wi-fi. In the Home Loans chapter, you'll see how I asked my Facebook friends if anyone has recently saved thousands by getting a better deal on their mortgage, and within 24 hours I had half a dozen great leads to add to what I could learn via online comparison sites.

True Story: Mikey Saves Around $600 By Asking Around

Michael Slezak is a senior journalist with the ABC and knows more than most about science, technology and the environment. But when Telstra whacked up his mobile charges, he turned to Twitter to vent:

← **Tweet**

Just got email from @Telstra saying they are increasing plan charges "in line with CPI". Are they increasing their wages and salaries in line with CPI too? (And would be nice if they dropped the loyalty tax too if they're doing this.)

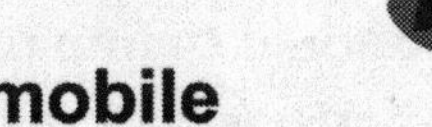

Your mobile plans and prices are changing.

I added my two-cents-worth, commenting that Belong is owned by Telstra, operates on the same network, and costs a fraction of the price.

My fellow money-saving nerd Robert Bozinovski then chimed in too, recommending Boost Mobile because they have access to the full Telstra 4G network. Then came this:

Thanks for these replies! I've moved my partner's mobile to Boost - saving us like $600 a year for equivalent service.

Mikey hadn't even asked for advice, but he turned out to be a very good listener!

Online reviews

You can also take the tips of strangers – but be picky. At websites such as ProductReview.com.au, OzBargain.com.au and CHOICE.com.au, a mixture of experts and amateurs give their views on all sorts of products, including most household bills.

These can be a useful touchpoint – particularly when the reviews are by experts (as in the case of CHOICE, which is why you have to pay for them) or by complete amateurs on a non-profit basis (as in the case of OzBargain, which is a large and very quirky online community of hardcore Bill-Killers who swap notes about everything from KFC specials to electric vehicles!).

But you should take some online review sites with a grain of salt. Your electricity provider has bad reviews? Check out some other electricity providers' reviews before you jump to too many conclusions – you'll find they almost all have bad reviews. (People just don't like electricity companies. They've even been compared to cigarette companies in reputational research, which I think is a bit rough.)

INSIDE INFO

Some review sites are also being gamed. Any business that cares enough about online reviews will have people working behind the scenes on generating positive reviews, so the best-reviewed providers are sometimes just the best-resourced. In fact, the way some of these sites make a buck is by going to businesses and saying, 'We can help you improve your reviews for a fee.' So don't believe everything you read online (as if I needed to tell you that!).

CHAPTER 10
THE SQUEAKY WHEEL

As the old saying goes, 'the squeaky wheel gets the oil', and unfortunately it's often true.

If you don't ask for a better deal, and you don't officially complain when things go wrong, you're unlikely to get the best possible results.

This doesn't mean you have to be a serial complainant, forever firing off cranky emails and social posts (there are already enough of those 'trolls' out there who put *way* too much time into their whingeing).

What it does mean is that if you want to get a result from a large company with thousands of customers, you need to master the art of the 'Squeaky Wheel' and learn to 'whinge well'.

There are three escalating steps to being an effective whinger:

1. Whinge to the boss,
2. Whinge in public, and
3. Whinge to the regulator.

Each time you try one and don't get a result, you should take it to the next step.

STEP 1: Whinge to the boss

The trick to the 'Squeaky Wheel' is to get your complaint noticed by someone as high on the tree as you possibly can.

Your complaint is like one of those little penguins in the David Attenborough docos, competing with hundreds of other penguins to climb out of the roiling ocean without being dashed against the rocks before it can make it to the front of the queue.

I've been a manager who sometimes had to take calls about people's complaints, and the fact is that if one of our million-plus members had an issue at One Big Switch and they got through to me, they probably had a better chance of a rapid resolution.

Why? I usually take personal responsibility for the case and I ask my team to help me resolve it ASAP. I don't see a lot of these cases, unlike the member services team who deal with inquiries all day, so the ones I do see stand out to me.

Big businesses are the same, multiplied by a hundred. With them, you really need to make your penguin stand out somehow!

So if you complain and you don't get a fair result immediately, ask for it to be escalated to a manager and tell them why you think it's unfair.

A Telstra customer told me she once wrote directly to the CEO about her problem. Because he has a team of people monitoring his correspondence, she got a result quick smart – probably much quicker than if she'd started at the bottom!

Another good tip I've heard is to use the human resources site LinkedIn.com. Like Facebook for people's work lives, it allows you to search by company and find the names and job titles of all the people who work for an organisation. So, if you're the resourceful type, you might be able to locate the *exact* person who can fix your problem, and drop them a little note to say hi.

But for goodness' sake, *be polite*. Be reasonable. Bear in mind it's just someone doing their job. People are much more likely to go into bat for you if you're not an arsehole.

But if that doesn't work ...

STEP 2: Whinge in public

Once upon a time, cranky customers who couldn't get their complaints resolved used to stand outside the business's front office with a sandwich board strapped to their chest. Some still do!

But the internet has been a wonderful development for both complainants and businesses – if not for the makers of sandwich boards. You can now rabble-rouse from the comfort of your own home and it can be just as effective.

The most common way to make a complaint public now is by posting it on social media.

Facebook, Twitter, Instagram and TikTok are the new 'shop window'. Most businesses resolve social media complaints as a priority because they don't like their dirty laundry hanging out in public. Big businesses have whole teams of people who just monitor comments and try to resolve them ASAP.

If Step #1 didn't resolve your issue, post a comment on the business's Facebook and Instagram pages and tag them in a tweet (if you're on Twitter).

Here's an example from when my broadband service went down and I couldn't get a resolution on phone or live chat:

Earth to @Optus - can't get through on phone, live chat or carrier pigeon to ask why my broadband service has been down for 24hrs, so trying Twitter. Is there anyone home?

5:31 PM - 10 Jan 2018

2 Retweets 1 Like

2 2 1

Once again, *be polite*. If you're rude on social media, there's nowhere to hide. Everyone can see you being a crank. (But a lame joke or two? That's perfectly OK.)

INSIDE INFO Facebook has a very clever button for businesses that allows them to 'hide' your comment from all but you and your 'friends'. So the ruder you are, the less likely others are to end up seeing your complaint.

If nonc of the above works, it's time to ...

STEP 3: Whinge to the regulator

When my wi-fi went down for a month, I tried both steps one and two above.

When I asked for compensation via my provider's live chat service, someone called Noah told me it was not their fault but the local electricity network's, and *he* lost his temper at *me*.

I also complained extensively on Twitter, but it was like whingeing in space, where no one can hear you scream.

But then my wife gave me a great tip. (Remember how being a good listener is one of the secrets to saving on your bills?)

In Australia, if you make an official complaint to the national Telecommunications Industry Ombudsman ('TIO' to his mates), your provider has to open a file for your complaint and allocate someone internally to resolve it.

Many other industries operate similar processes for complaints.

So I complained to my new best mate TIO. Here's what happened next:

- On 25 January I told the ombudsman I wanted the provider to: 'Restore service ASAP. Communicate with customers the progress of the fix regularly. Refund the month's broadband fees. Refund the month's mobile fees too (I am having to tether from my Optus mobile and using up all my data to cover the lack of wi-fi).'

- On 29 January, the ombudsman wrote to say they'd relayed the complaint to the provider.
- On 5 February, the wi-fi came back on and the provider called to say they would refund the month's wi-fi charges and the excess data charges on my mobile.
- And on 2 March, they contacted me to say they were crediting our account another $459.80 as compensation for the inconvenience!

You never know, but I think if I hadn't been a squeaky wheel and taken the complaint to the official channels, we wouldn't have gotten this result.

Unfortunately, sometimes it pays to be difficult. But it also pays to do it the EASIEST way possible – after all, who wants to stand around all day with a sandwich board strapped to them?!

INSIDE INFO

John Rolfe writes the 'Public Defender' column at the *Daily Telegraph*, where he takes up the cause of readers who've been dudded and tries to get their money back for them. His advice is:

> *'Call once, write once, then take it to a higher power if you don't get a result – the relevant ombudsman, regulator or consumer tribunal. Don't engage in a tit-for-tat. Your initial letter should contain:*
>
> - *The issue*
> - *What you want them to do about it*
> - *A reasonable deadline for action*
> - *What you will do if they don't take action (e.g. "I intend to take my complaint to the ombudsman if it's not resolved in the manner and the time-frame described above."). And remember to attach relevant evidence, such as proof of purchase or an independent assessment of the problem.'*

Here's the wording of my complaint to TIO below. (As we'll see in the 'Red Dog' trick later, you shouldn't be afraid to ask for a lot of compensation. Ask for whatever you've missed out on, plus something extra for the inconvenience. Don't hold back.)

TIO Complaint #2018/01/17251

Complaint description	No internet service to the area for 15 days so far. No proactive communication from Optus as to what the issue is or when it will be fixed. Only a reply to a tweet on Jan 17 stating 'Hey Joel :) Thanks for that. I can see from the note on the fault number that we're working with the power company to get this resolved as quickly as possible. Still no ETR – Marie'. Ausgrid has tweeted saying its work is not preventing Optus from fixing the issue.
Your preferred outcome	Restore service ASAP. Communicate with customers the progress of the fix regularly. Refund the month's broadband fees. Refund the month's mobile fees too (I am using up all my Optus mobile data to cover the lack of wi-fi).

CHAPTER 11
DAVID'S SLINGSHOT

When pint-sized David took on Goliath, he was battling the Old Testament equivalent of Arnie Schwarzenegger or The Rock.

But David had two things going for him.

One, he was blessed by God (a handy leg-up in life). And two, he was also blessed by technology, in the form of a humble slingshot.

We might not think of a slingshot as technology, but in 1020 BC it was probably the taser of its time.

The Old Testament story is a reminder that humans are unique among the animal kingdom in our ability to make tools to tackle complex challenges.

When we needed to fight bigger creatures - human or otherwise - we created weapons.

When we needed to get somewhere, we created the wheel and then the chariot, the train, the car and finally the plane (and yes, the monorail, but no species is perfect...).

And then we created possibly the most significant human invention of all time: the internet.

The internet is your equivalent of David's slingshot - it will help you win battles you never could have attempted before.

When you want to save on your bills and you're negotiating with a big, billion-dollar business with thousands of employees, you can feel a bit like David taking on Goliath.

The main reason is that it's not usually a level playing field. You're suffering from what economists call 'information asymmetry' - the business knows all about electricity or insurance or home loans and has thousands of customers they can study to understand the typical consumer.

Then there's little old you.

But the internet has changed the game. The internet has made it easier than ever before to find the right information to level that playing field (as long as you know where to look, and we'll tell you that in the next part of this book).

Did you know, for example, that in most states there's a website that will tell you what the cheapest electricity deals are in your area and rank them in price order? In many cases you can just upload your last bill and it does the rest.

The traditional smoke and mirrors around home loans is now clearing too, thanks to a whole range of websites and tools that are putting it all out there for you to see.

A bit of smart internet research can save you hundreds or even thousands of dollars a year on your bills. And you can also switch online in minutes.

Don't have internet at home? Not super confident with it? Go to the local library or ask someone for help, and read the tips in the second half of this book.

Because without the web, you're like David meeting Goliath without a rock or a slingshot.

True Story: Valeria From Queensland Switches Health Funds And Saves $872 A Year . . . On Her Phone . . . At The Gym!

So you think switching your health insurance policy is complicated? That it takes hours on the phone and isn't worth the hassle?

Oh, ye of little faith! I give you Valeria from Queensland.

When we heard that a young mum in Queensland had saved $872 on her premium by switching to a new provider and plan, we were pretty chuffed.

But when we learnt that she'd done it entirely on her phone, while at the gym, we nearly fell out of our chairs!

'The switching process was very easy. I was actually at the gym and was able to fill out my form online on my phone, and it took, you know, just a few minutes,' Valeria said.

Valeria's a busy mum and photographer based on the Sunshine Coast.

After seeing one of our TV segments about the benefits of shopping around, she changed her health insurance to similar cover with a different fund and saved a whopping $872 a year on her base premium. She also got a $300 gift card as a bonus for joining the new fund.

'We were very close to dropping our cover because I was paying almost $400 a month, which is very, very expensive. So to cut that back was a huge saving for us and knowing that we have that peace of mind of cover is really important.'

When I checked in again with Valeria later, she told me she'd just switched again to another fund, and achieved even better value for her money. So lightning does strike twice.

CHAPTER 12
THE RED DOG

Like I said earlier, loyalty is all but dead in household bills. But it hasn't breathed its last gasp just yet. (Like Westley in *The Princess Bride*, it's just 'mostly dead'!)

I needed to include this final insider trick as an acknowledgment that there are indeed cases where it pays to be loyal.

I may be cynical but I'm not entirely one-eyed. And the 'Red Dog' is about showing loyalty to providers when (and *only* when) they show loyalty to you.

(I also needed to include this trick so I'd have an excuse to put a gratuitous picture of my dog in the book. This is Sunny the Money-Saving Dog. He's not red, but he's got some reddish patches. 'Mostly red', maybe!)

Dogs make us feel good about life, the universe and everything else, because they're so darn loyal – for better or worse.

Some of us are like that as consumers: so very, very loyal, even when our providers don't do the right thing by us.

I'll explain below why that's completely natural – in fact, it's *more* human to be loyal than it is to be disloyal.

And there are a few rare examples where businesses do show loyalty to customers who deserve it, which also makes me feel good about the world.

Hence this final insider trick: the 'Red Dog'.

Red Dog is one of Australia's favourite movies. It's in the top ten highest-grossing Aussie films of all time. Based on a true story and a book by Louis de Bernières, it's the story of a red kelpie without a master who attaches himself to John Grant, an American truck driver working in a WA iron ore mine.

When John has a motorbike accident and doesn't come home one day, Red Dog waits for him for weeks, and then goes out looking for him, covering much of Australia's vast Pilbara region between Perth and Darwin and even – according to one rumour – jumping a ship to Japan.

In the end, Red Dog dies lying next to John's grave and there's now a statue erected in his memory in Dampier, WA.

© Peter Ptschelinzew / Alamy

What does all that have to do with your latest bill?

Well, 'doing a Red Dog' is a calculated tactic whereby you go all-in with your loyalty to one provider, because the rewards are worth it.

I want to be clear that these cases are rare: usually, the *best* way to kill bills is to fight our own human nature, adopt the 'De Niro' attitude I've described earlier, embrace change and be ruthlessly disloyal.

As a general rule, rewards and loyalty programs have a higher 'perceived value' than their real value. They cost the business LESS than real discounts, and that's why they all seem to offer them these days – instead of just offering the lowest prices

But there are indeed times where a business will reward you for your loyalty, and sometimes it makes perfect sense to give them loyalty in return.

So here are some examples:

Supermarkets

Petrol discounts: Spend $30 at Coles or Woolies and you'll earn petrol discount vouchers, which you can cash in for a 4 cents per litre discount at participating fuel outlets. Sometimes you can also 'stack' them with other promotions or discounted gift cards to get up to 20c/L off.

Verdict: *Perhaps not surprisingly, Coles and Woolies' fuel outlets often sell petrol at about 4c/L more than the little independent outlets, so using these dockets can just make your petrol as cheap as the cheaper stations. But if that works for you, do it! The reality is, you need to hunt out the cheapest petrol in your area using a kit-bag of discount vouchers, petrol apps and inside info – and some days that kit-bag will tell you that the best deal is 4c/L off at Shell Coles Express.*

Rewards programs: Coles and Woolies also have very sophisticated rewards programs called Flybuys and Everyday Rewards that are designed to keep you within their universe of stores and collect data about your habits that makes them better at selling to you. They reward you for using their supermarkets, their discount department stores, their bottle shops, their petrol stations, their credit cards, their insurance and their telco products.

Verdict: *At the most basic level, you have to spend $2000 at Coles or Woolies supermarkets to earn a $10 discount on your next shop, which ain't much of a reward. But these schemes are designed to multiply your rewards by up to six or seven times if you're prepared to use all of the services above. Again: you're better off being a Lone Ranger and looking for the best deal on each service. But if you lived in a one-supermarket, one-servo, one-bottleshop town, for example, and they were all owned by the same company, you'd be mad not to go the full 'Red Dog'. Or if you're a dedicated rewards hunter, chasing bonus points and 'gaming' the algorithm, some savvy money-savers say it can save them around $1000 a year. It really depends on your personal circumstances.*

Health insurance

Bonus limits: Some health funds will give you higher claim limits if you've been with them for longer. For example, your annual limit for dental might be $1000 in year one, but if you've been a member for five years, they'll increase it to $1200. Or you might be able to claim up to $50 per dental check-up, and that increases to $70 after a few years. Note that these bonus limits almost always apply to 'extras' treatments such as dental, orthodontic, physio and optometry – not to hospital treatments.

Verdict: *Nice-to-have, and these bonuses might mean there's nothing as generous when you shop around. But not a reason to stay with a health fund if the base premium and the cover you're getting are not good value in themselves.*

Home & car insurance

Multi-policy discounts: Providers who sell multiple products can sometimes reward you for taking out more than one policy with them. You might get an extra 10 or 15% off your home insurance premium, for example, if you also have car insurance and/or landlord's insurance with the same company.

Verdict: *If you like the product and the price to begin with, this can be a real bonus. But don't take out a policy at a price that's not competitive and then rely on the multi-policy discount to make it better. Also, don't just assume they add up to more than the savings you'll get from shopping around. Often the starting price is high, so the multi-policy discount just brings your total back down to earth. (See the section on Home & Car Insurance later.) Finally, businesses regularly change their policy on this one, I've found, so do check from time to time to see if you're still getting these savings.*

Telcos

Bundling discounts: A bit like a multi-policy discount on insurance, telcos often give you a discount on the second or third product you take out with them. I used to get $20 a month off my mobile plan because I had broadband with the same company, for example.

Verdict: *Again, a good rule is that the price and product have to be competitive before the bundled discount, otherwise the bundle can become a trap that just locks you into more than one over-priced product. Later, we'll see how you can get most of the elements in a Telstra bundle for about $600 a year less – if you're prepared to compromise.*

Case Study: Red Dog Versus De Niro

Are you better off giving all your business to one loyalty scheme and trying to maximise the payback? Or shopping around for the cheapest prices and paying no heed to points?

It's a perennial question, and it's not an easy one to answer.

Rewards points don't have an intrinsic value: a Qantas point, for example, is worth about 2c on average, according to Finder.com.au. But it ranges from 0.5c if exchanged for gift cards, right up to about 5c if used to redeem first class upgrades.

So it's impossible to calculate precisely the value of a rewards scheme for a 'typical' household – not only because of the elusive value of points but also because of the profusion of 'bonus point offers' each scheme produces.

But it is at least possible to add up how many base points you'd earn by doing your grocery shopping, petrol, car and home insurance and a rewards credit card with one program – and to calculate the dollar value based on the average value of a point. So that's what I did for one newspaper column.

My imaginary household spends $300 a week on groceries, $100 on fuel, $35 a month on a mobile plan and $2000 a year on car and home insurance. I looked at Coles, Woolies and Qantas as the major examples, as of late 2022:

Coles

Use a Coles rewards credit card (annual fee $99) to pay for the groceries: 600 Flybuys points. Take out Coles car and home insurance with the card: another 600 bonus grocery points each week, plus 4000 points for the premiums. Take out a Coles Mobile plan: get 10% off one shop a month (worth $30). And $2 in fuel docket savings a week.

TOTAL: About $858 a year in base rewards for $23,000 spend. (Plus $320 in bonus points for taking out the new Coles financial products, but that's a one-off.)

Woolies

Woolies was not accepting new credit card applications but based on its most recent rewards card offer: 600-900 Everyday Rewards points for your weekly grocery shop, plus 2000 points for your car and home insurance premiums. Woolworths Mobile plan: 10% off one shop a month (worth $30), and fuel dockets about $2 a week.

TOTAL: About $790 a year in base rewards for $23,000 spend. (Both Flybuys and Everyday Rewards points are worth on average about 0.5c each.)

Qantas

Use a Qantas rewards card (annual fee $249) to pay for your groceries and you'll get 300 Qantas points. You'll also get 2000 Qantas points for using it to pay Qantas car and home insurance premiums, and another 2000 for taking out those policies. Qantas has a deal with BP that offers similar value to the supermarket dockets: $2/week.

TOTAL: About $496 in base rewards for a $22,500 spend. (Plus a one-off $2000 in bonus points for taking out the new Qantas products.)

So my imaginary household gets around $500-$900 in base value from being loyal, and maybe the same again if they play the rewards game and chase bonus point deals. To work out if they're in front, you'd need to decide if they're spending that much extra by sticking with one provider rather than shopping around. (Shopping at Aldi, for example, can save you upwards of 10% a year according to comparisons by CHOICE and others.)

CONSUMER PSYCHOLOGY 101: Why it's only human to want to be loyal

If you find it hard to act like Robert De Niro, you're only human. Most of us do!

Social scientists have proven that, as human beings, we prefer inertia to most forms of change – even when change is in our best interests.

This is because of two essential human traits that psychologists and economists have shown to be prevalent in experiment after experiment: they call them 'status quo bias' and 'loss aversion'.

'Loss aversion' is our curious tendency to feel losses more than we feel wins. The boffins estimate that losing something makes us twice as miserable as gaining something makes us happy.

A collection of Nobel Prize-winning economists have tested this with university students. They gave half of them a free mug and then asked them how much they'd be willing to give up the mug for. They also asked the students without mugs to say what they'd be willing to pay for a mug.

The students who had mugs wanted roughly twice the amount for their mugs than the other students were prepared to pay for them.

'Thousands of mugs have been used in dozens of replications of this experiment, but the results are nearly always the same,' writes one of the economists, Professor Richard Thaler, in his best-selling book *Nudge: Improving Decisions about Health, Wealth and Happiness*. 'Once I have a mug, I don't want to give it up. But if I don't have one, I don't feel an urgent need to buy one.'

In another experiment, half the class got mugs and half got chocolate bars worth the same amount. When asked if they wanted to switch, only one in ten students said yes.

Our 'status quo bias' is similar but not quite the same.

As human beings, we tend towards the status quo and avoid change unless it's really necessary. 'Better the devil you know', as the saying goes. There's example after example of this.

TV programmers know that if you win the 6pm news slot or the 7.30pm entertainment slot, you'll often go on to win the ratings for the rest of the evening. Because people prefer not to change the channel!

When streaming services give you a free trial, it's because they know that once they have your payment details, many of us won't cancel after a month, even if we're not using the service much.

Australians have about $670 billion in so-called 'MySuper' superannuation funds, which is the default fund regulated by government. Some of us may actively choose those funds, but most are probably just leaving them in the default fund because of status quo bias.

Put loss aversion, status quo bias and household bills together and what do you get?

Inertia! Blind loyalty! Laziness! Ripped off!

Those are just some of the words that get thrown around to explain why we don't switch and save more often.

Call it what you like – it's a very human response and if we want to pay as little as possible for our bills and save that money to spend on other things that make us and our families happy, we need to understand our own human nature and know when to fight against it.

Businesses know about loss aversion and status quo bias and they use them to sell us stuff. Politicians know about loss aversion and status quo bias and they use them to try and win our vote, or create scare campaigns about their rivals.

We need to know about them too, if only because everybody else does! And when it comes to finding the easiest savings, a bit of self-knowledge goes a long way.

P.S. 'Grandfathered' deals deserve the Red Dog treatment too

There's another example where it pays to be loyal: sometimes you're on a cracking deal they don't offer anymore and you'd be a mug to leave!

These so-called 'grandfathered' deals can be better than anything currently on the market because the market might have gone backwards since you locked them in, but the provider may be prepared to keep offering you the same product unless you decide to change.

So you have to apply some common sense: don't move for the sake of moving. Just be ready to.

True Story: I Couldn't Save My Brother Any Money On His Health Insurance. Sorry, Bro!

In case you think I'm suggesting you'll save hundreds of dollars every time you so much as glance at another product or provider, here's the sorry tale of my recent attempt to help my brother save a few bucks on his health insurance.

My bro is a regular switcher; he shops around and moves when he sees a good deal, so he doesn't usually need any help from me.

But he did ask me once to take a look at some health insurance deals suggested to him by a comparison website, so I did.

What I found was that they couldn't beat the policy he was on for value. They were proposing a downgrade to save money, but it would have meant getting rid of some cover he wanted to keep.

He was on a plan that no longer exists (probably because it's far better than anything that's now available). The fund was probably losing money on him if he ever needed to claim, but they had decided to keep giving him that plan for as long as he wanted it.

Once we realised that, he decided it was best to stay put on this occasion.

So there you go – sometimes you are better off remaining loyal.

So there you have it.

We've just run through the 9 key insider tricks I've picked up over the years that you need to master if you want to pay bottom dollar for your bills.

We've also looked at some of the basic human traits of consumer psychology 101 that we have to battle against to be an effective

Bill-Killer. The path to eternal money-saving happiness is going to mean you need to keep the following in mind:

- Be a 'Price-Chaser' not a 'Sleeping Beauty'.
- Don't get paralysed by all the choice out there! Remember that 'good enough' is almost always good enough.
- Always have another offer to 'anchor' your negotiations with providers.
- Don't be afraid of change, or of losing things that aren't really that valuable anyway.
- Save your loyalty for those providers who show it to *you* first.

You've now got all the theory you need to kick some serious household bill backside. So let's move on to the more practical stuff: the inside info you need to know about each bill, how to get a quick win and find the easy money, and then how to win over and over again throughout your lifetime.

Because no matter how good you are at keeping them under control, bills are like cane toads – they have a tendency to just keep on coming!

PART 3

A BILL-BY-BILL BREAKDOWN (AND WHERE TO FIND THE EASY MONEY)

If there's one vital money lesson I've learnt in the past few years, it's how much easy money is out there, just waiting for us to claim it back.

This is OUR money, but it just happens to be sitting in the coffers of Australian governments and businesses we've dealt with.

Sometimes they have it because we've paid them more than we should have. Sometimes it's because they've been unable to contact us. But whatever the reason, we're going to get it back for you. And it won't be that hard.

In fact, the easiest dollar you'll ever earn is the dollar that's already sitting on the table, just waiting for you to pick it up.

The first part of this book outlined 7 Simple Steps for picking the low-hanging fruit from the easy money tree. This part of the book goes into more depth to help you pick off every last apple, year after year.

So let's start with what I call FREE Money, or money for nothing. These are the dollars we can claim back with a few easy keystrokes or a bit of help from some free experts.

CHAPTER 13
FREE MONEY!

'Money won is twice as sweet as money earned.'
Paul Newman in *The Color of Money*

At my last count, Australian governments, the tax office, banks and super funds were holding over $20 billion of OUR money. This is how much they're sitting on:

Governments	Super Funds & The Tax Office	Banks

$2.5 billion	$13.8 billion	$5 billion

You could be entitled to hundreds or thousands of dollars from these pots. Even if none of it's yours, you might find a small windfall for friends and family. And it's so easy to check if you're entitled to any of this 'money for nothing'.

If you've only got a few minutes to find free money, just run through the 'Unclaimed money', 'Lost super' and 'Cashback' sections below. That's where the easiest wins are to be found. If you've got a bit more time, tackle 'Bank refunds'.

In a nutshell

Potential saving	Anywhere from $0–$1 million!
Easiest	'Unclaimed money', 'Lost super' and 'Cashback websites'
Next-easiest	'Junk insurance refunds' and 'Financial advice refunds'
Top tools	Government 'unclaimed money' websites and 'lost super' sites, plus cashback websites such as Cashrewards.com.au
If I could tell you one thing about 'free money' it would be:	It's your money. Governments and banks are just 'minding' it for you. Because it's yours, they won't fight hard for it. Go get it.

UNCLAIMED MONEY

Potential windfall: Anywhere from $0–$1 million!

The federal government is holding over $1.5 billion of other people's money; NSW has over $450 million of our money, Queensland is sitting on more than $150 million, and Victoria won't say how much it has, but it's also in the 'hundreds of millions'.

Why? When a business, council or government agency tries to send you money and you don't receive it, for whatever reason, it ends up in consolidated revenue as 'unclaimed money'.

Examples might include: refunds and overpayments from a purchase; sale of property, goods or services; deposits and premiums; principal and interest; share dividends; uncashed or undeposited cheques; trust account funds; commissions; royalties; inheritances and public sector superannuation.

The same thing happens with cash in bank accounts that remain untouched for seven or more years. (Julia Gillard's government reduced that timeframe to three years, arguing that the unclaimed money was just being eaten up by bank fees. But Tony Abbott's government then returned it to seven years, claiming that 'about 156,000 accounts worth $550 million a year were being effectively confiscated by the government'.)

So it turns out this happens quite a lot! And sometimes the amounts are staggering.

True Story: The Battle For Maria's Million

The largest pile of unclaimed money in Australia belonged to former PoW Maria Okinczyc, who died childless in 2001, leaving behind $1.07 million in assets. *The Daily Telegraph* investigated the case in 2021 and found that she arrived in Australia in 1949, bought a home with her (also since deceased) husband that was later sold and left multiple wills:

> *'Descendants in Italy have been attempting to claim the funds through "Money Detective" Peter King of Melbourne. Mr King has been working on the case for four years. He has found multiple wills in that time. In a recent breakthrough, the Italian descendants have agreed to split the money with two sets of Mrs Okinczyc's friends, all now in their 90s, who were named in a 1982 will.'*

For most of us, of course, any windfalls are going to be much smaller than Mrs Okinczyc's fortune. But checking for them is a piece of cake, so if you've never done it, it's a no-brainer. Most state and federal governments have an online form you can plug your name into to see if any of the money belongs to you. If you see an amount you think is yours, you can stake a claim. You'll need to produce some documentation to prove it's you – for example, an old bill showing you lived at a certain address.

PRO TIP

Search BOTH federal and state government sites. If you've lived in other states (or even if you haven't) it's a good idea to check those state government sites too.

You should also search for friends and family, especially your late relatives who cannot search for themselves.

There's no time limit on claims so go back as far as you like.

Where To Search

FEDERAL: Search 'ASIC unclaimed money' on Google
ACT: Search 'ACT Public Trustee and Guardian unclaimed money'
NSW: Search 'Revenue NSW unclaimed money'
NT: Search 'Northern Territory Treasury unclaimed money'
QLD: Search 'Public Trustee of Queensland unclaimed money'
SA: Search 'South Australian Department of Treasury unclaimed money'
TAS: Search 'Tasmanian Department of Treasury and Finance unclaimed money' or phone (03) 6166 4188
VIC: Search 'State Revenue Office of Victoria unclaimed money'
WA: Search 'WA Department of Treasury unclaimed money'

Unfortunately, I found nothing for myself when I searched, but I did find an easy $1500 for my dad.

I've also had a bit of fun searching on behalf of a few famous names over the years. So if you come across any of the following, be sure to let them know there's some easy money on the table for them!

Clive Palmer: $228 with Westpac
Scott and Jenny Morrison: $609.87 with St George
Richard Pratt: $4300 from ANZ
Kevin Rudd: $1515 from PayPal

CASHBACK WEBSITES

Potential saving: $100s a year

Before the internet, businesses sometimes paid other businesses a commission if they sent them a customer. A life insurance company would pay a financial adviser for sending them a client, for example, or a car salesman might pay a 'finder's fee' to a mechanic.

The internet made these kickbacks the rule, not the exception. Most businesses that sell stuff online now pay other businesses for 'clicks' or 'leads' sent to their website – because they're so easy to automatically track in a digital world.

What the new breed of cashback website does is this: it gives some of that kickback BACK to you. All you need to do is visit one of their thousands of partner businesses via the cashback website or use a linked card and if you buy something, the cashback is credited to your account.

The average cashback is about 7%, but they have short-term specials or 'boosted cashback offers' that regularly go up to 20% or 30% with some retailers. Occasionally you'll even see 50% cashback up to a certain limit.

So that you don't need to go to the cashback site every time you want to buy something online, they've created automatic 'notifiers' that appear in your browser when you're searching to tell you how much each business is paying in cashback. There's an example below from my search for kids school shoes.

How To Really Cash In On Cashback

- Join at least one, if not both, of the major cashback sites: Cashrewards and ShopBack.
- Link the card you use most to both websites so that you'll also get cashback for in-store purchases, not just online ones.
- Download the 'notifier' in 'settings' so that you'll see what cashback is available when searching for something online.

- Keep an eye on their emails or websites such as OzBargain.com.au to see which 'boosted cashback offers' are coming each week.

PRO TIP

Look for 'cashback stacks' where you can combine a big cashback deal with a sale. The cashback stack is the money-saving equivalent of being 'kicked up the arse by a rainbow', as Barnaby Joyce would say. Marketing types are flat out trying to sell their products and sometimes they don't notice when they're BOTH offering a big discount on an item and ALSO a kickback to anyone who sends them a customer. So you might be able to combine say 30% off with 20% cashback, which would add to an effective discount of 44%.

True Story: How I Paid $72 For A $110 Pair Of School Shoes

When my boy needed new shoes for school, I googled 'black school shoes' and a list of sellers came up with little purple and red notifications telling me how much cashback I could get from each shoe seller.

That's because I have the 'plug-in' notifiers for cashback websites installed on my laptop. I highly recommend downloading them.

Here's what the search results looked like:

The Home Of School Shoes - Shop The Biggest Range

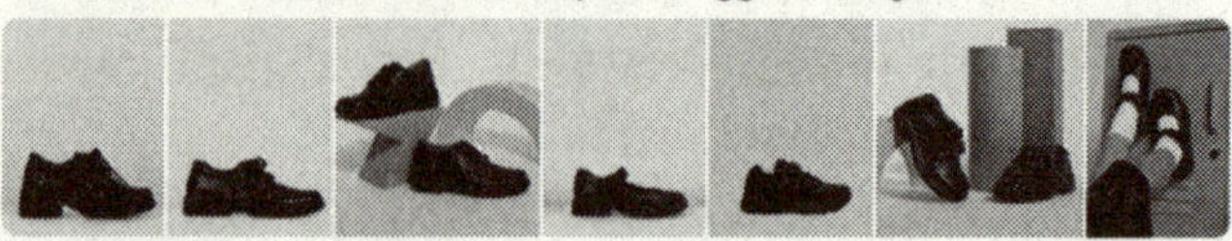

Home of the Fit Squad - the experts in **school shoes**. Shop Clarks, Pablosky, Roc & more. Free shipping & Afterpay. ... style-**black** sport ...

Primary School Shoes · High School Shoes · School · Lace Up

https://www.target.com.au › school › school-shoes
Earn Up to 3.50% cashback at Target
Get Up to 2.8% Cashback via Shopback
School Shoes - Target Australia
15 products — Shop a great range of kids **school shoes** including **black** leather shoes for girls and boys at Target Australia. Check out our Free Delivery offer.

I scrolled down and saw that ASICS had a sale on plus 12% cashback via Cashrewards, so I clicked through, found a pair on sale and ended up paying $72.60 for a $110 pair of shoes. Winning!

(They should fit him for about a month until he grows another two shoe sizes and then I'll do the whole thing all over again.)

LOST SUPER

Potential windfall: Anywhere from $0 to $1000s

The downside of compulsory super (apart from the fact that you can't touch 10% of your income until you're in your 60s) is that Australians have almost $14 billion of it sitting in lost and unclaimed accounts.

If you've ever changed your name, address, job or lived overseas, you might have lost some of your super.

At one point, the average Aussie had FOUR accounts floating around - and probably didn't know it - because in the old days, they'd open a new account for you every time you changed jobs.

The problem with this was that you paid fees and sometimes insurance premiums out of every account, which occasionally ate away the entire balance.

So they changed the law in 2019 to make sure inactive accounts with low balances are now transferred to the tax office. If your balance is less than $6,000 and there are no contributions or roll-overs for 16 continuous months, it'll be transferred.

The tax office then has the power to pro-actively merge your super accounts if it can do so. They've also made it much easier for you to roll them all into one account online with no paperwork.

Here are the latest numbers:

- 4 million Aussies have two or more super accounts.
- In 2020 alone we found and consolidated almost $7 BILLION of lost super.
- The average balance of second and third accounts is unknown but given there's about $14 billion of unclaimed super out there, spread between 4 million of us, it could be in the vicinity of $3500.

Here's how to find out if some of it is yours.

OPTION 1: D.I.Y.

1. Log into your MyGov account.
2. Click through to the 'Australian Taxation Office' link.
3. Scroll down to the 'Super' section and click on 'Manage my Super'.

STOP!

Before transferring your super, ASIC says you should check the following (and if you have any questions, ask a financial adviser – your super fund might have one, for example):

- Is the fund with the bigger balance better? You might be better off moving it all to the smaller account.
- Will changing funds affect how much your employer contributes? Some employers contribute more to certain funds.
- Do you have any insurance through the fund? If so, can you get the same cover with the new fund? 'Be particularly careful if you have a pre-existing medical condition or are aged 60 or over.'
- Tell your employers so they're paying into the right account.
- Check your type of super fund: they can either be accumulation or defined benefits funds. If you are in a defined benefits super fund get professional advice before you leave.

OPTION 2: D.I.F.M. (DO IT FOR ME)

Registered tax agents and super funds can also find and consolidate your super accounts for you. For example, if you want to roll multiple balances into your main super account, you could contact your super fund and they'll help you do so. (Chances are, they've already contacted you about this multiple times, but letters from super funds are like books about money – not enough people read them!)

You can also ask your accountant for help, if you have one.

REMEDIATION SERVICES

Potential windfall: Anywhere from $0 to $20,000

In 2018, there was a Banking Royal Commission that revealed billions of dollars of rip-offs and dodgy practices in the financial services industry.

Some of the worst examples involved dead people being charged fees for financial advice and unemployed people being charged insurance premiums to cover them 'if they lost their job'.

As a result, Australia's banks and wealth management companies put aside over $5 billion for 'consumer remediation' to be given back to customers.

This was an acknowledgment on their part that all that money was ours, not theirs – we'd paid it to them when we shouldn't have.

Billions have been refunded already, but now it's up to us to claim back the billions still remaining, which is easier said than done. For starters, millions of us probably still have no idea that some of our money is sitting there. Even if we do, we might not have the know-how or the confidence to claim it back.

There are two main pots of money that banks have put aside: junk insurance refunds and financial advice refunds. There are free and easy ways to check them both, so read on.

POT #1: JUNK INSURANCE

Over the past decade, the big banks and major insurance companies have sold over 5.6 million policies for so-called 'junk insurance' on credit cards and loans. That's more than one policy for every four Australian adults! In many cases, the customer didn't even know what they were signing up for – or thought it was compulsory.

'Junk insurance' is an umbrella term for a range of insurance policies that were sometimes added to credit cards and loans. It's not cheap – some policies can cost over $2000 a year and you might get absolutely no benefit from them.

The official term is 'add-on insurance' but they've become known as 'junk' for a range of reasons:

- If you weren't aware of the cover and what it included or excluded, chances are it was 'mis-sold'; or
- They might have signed you up using dodgy sales tactics; or
- It might be entirely worthless to you. Some policies are double-ups of insurance we already have elsewhere, or they 'cover' us for things that are automatically covered anyway under consumer law, or we're not even eligible for them for some reason or other.

HOW DO YOU KNOW IF YOU'VE PAID FOR JUNK INSURANCE?

The clues could be in your old credit card or loan statements. You can request your old statements from any financial institution and search for something that looks like the insurances below, or you can ask a free consumer remediation service to chase it down for you (details below).

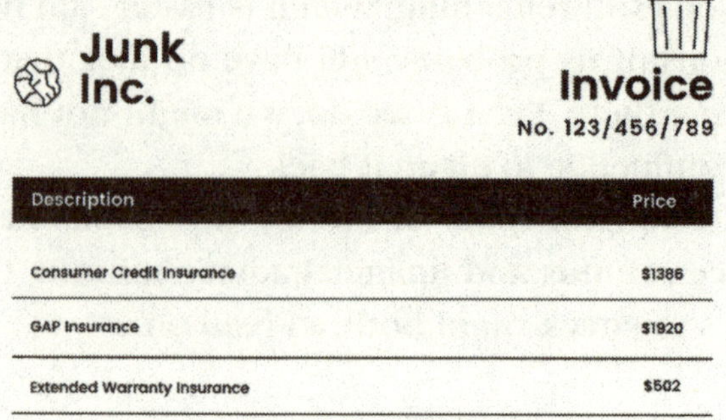

Description	Price
Consumer Credit Insurance	$1386
GAP Insurance	$1920
Extended Warranty Insurance	$502

THE MOST COMMON TYPES OF 'JUNK INSURANCE'

Consumer Credit Insurance (also known as CCI): This was added to credit cards, personal loans, car loans and home loans. It provides cover if you're unable to meet your minimum monthly repayments due to unemployment, sickness or injury, or to pay an outstanding loan balance if you die. But the Royal Commission exposed how many of these policies were sold to people who were ineligible to claim or unlikely to benefit or need cover.

Guaranteed Asset Protection (also known as GAP Insurance): Let's say you have a car accident and you have $17,000 owing on your car loan, but your car is written off and your comprehensive insurance policy only pays out $15,000. GAP Insurance is designed to cover the gap between what you owe under your car loan and what your car insurer will pay. But if you don't have comprehensive insurance, then you shouldn't have been sold GAP Insurance.

Extended Warranty Insurance (also known as MBI or Mechanical Breakdown Insurance): Extended Warranty Insurance is where the consumer pays a fee in return for the warranty provider agreeing to repair or replace parts or components of goods in the event of defects or failures. But it's almost completely worthless on second-hand vehicles because it contains so many exclusions. Further, Australia's Consumer Law contains protections for your rights when it comes to the quality of parts, so therefore buying extended warranties is not necessary.

The other way to know if you might be a victim is to see if you've been a customer of this list of insurance companies identified by ASIC and the Royal Commission.

EVER HAD A POLICY WITH ANY OF THESE INSURERS?

- Aioi Nissay Dowa Insurance Company Australia (sells Toyota Insurance)
- NM Insurance (underwrites motorcycle insurance forThe Holland Insurance Company, AAI (part of Suncorp) and AIG Australia)

- Eric Insurance (formerly AVEA Insurance)
- LFI (insurer for Liberty Finance)
- Sovereign Insurance
- Virginia Surety
- QBE Insurance
- MTA Insurance (owned by Suncorp)
- Swann Insurance
- Allianz Insurance
- National Warranty Company

POT #2: FINANCIAL ADVICE REFUNDS (A.K.A. 'FEES FOR NO SERVICE')

These refunds are not as common as junk insurance, but they're usually bigger. The Royal Commission also exposed that the big banks, major super funds and wealth management companies charged Australians billions of dollars in fees for financial advice we probably never received.

These fees were often automatically deducted from our bank accounts or super funds, sometimes without us knowing.

For example, maybe you had an allocated financial adviser and you paid an annual fee, but they didn't deliver any real 'ongoing financial advice'. One meeting in six years? Not good enough. A brief meeting or phone call every year? Again, not good enough! A 'thorough review of the customer's financial needs' has to be conducted annually to charge a fee.

Or maybe you didn't have a financial adviser but you were still slugged with annual fees anyway. The adviser might have retired or died (or maybe YOU retired or your relative died and you've inherited their estate), but the fees kept coming out every year. If so, the fees were dodgy.

LANGUAGE TO LOOK FOR IN YOUR OLD STATEMENTS:

- Statement of Advice (SoA)
- Record of Advice (RoA)
- Financial Advice
- 'Ongoing general support services'
- Plan Service Fees
- Adviser Service Fees

GET A FREE REFUND CHECK FROM THE EXPERTS

In recent years I've done some work with Remediator, a leading consumer remediation service, helping them to get the word out about what I call 'Royal Commission Refunds'.

They run a free eligibility check for you at Remediator.com if you don't want to do all the legwork yourself. If they find a potential refund, they'll chase it down and then negotiate hard with the bank for you. If they succeed, their fee is a proportion of the refund.

There are about half a dozen services that now do this for consumers.

There are also various class actions underway, which you should have heard about if you're a part of them (Australia has an 'opt out' system that 'joins' you to a class action automatically, unless you choose to opt out).

Of course, you can always do it yourself if you have the time and the confidence. Even if you start out with the DIY approach and hit a wall, you can then call in the experts later on.

True Stories: Carmel And My Gran Got $1000s Back

Carmel from Birtinya, QLD, scored a refund of $19,794 for 'mis-sold' consumer credit insurance she started paying on a credit card 18 years ago.

'I was buying a house with them and so of course they were throwing everything at me, and they said "we just believe that this insurance would be good for you",' she told *7News*.

The key to the biggest refunds is interest – if you've been paying a junk insurance premium for years, you could be entitled to a full refund PLUS interest.

STOP THE PRESS! I've been banging the drum about bank refunds for over a year, but I've only just learned that my dear late gran was a victim too.

As this book was going to press, I heard from my dad that he'd been contacted by her former bank saying they had around $20,000 in refunded financial advice fees and interest to give back to the beneficiaries of her estate.

Like so many others, she was charged an annual fee and got nothing in return. What a disgrace. My gran passed away more than a decade ago, so she'll never see that money and the sad thing is, if the bank hadn't been able to contact her estate for whatever reason, her children might never have seen it either. I wonder how many other families are in this same boat.

CHAPTER 14
ENERGY

> 'Money doesn't make you happy. I now have $50 million but I was just as happy when I had $48 million.'
> **Arnold Schwarzenegger, who clearly has too much money!**

Australia, land of more coal, gas, sun and wind per head of capita than any other country on the face of the earth, should have the cheapest power bills in the world. They should be giving the stuff away!

Instead, we've had crisis after crisis over two decades, which produced some of the world's priciest energy.

First, electricity bills doubled from 2007 to 2017 (see the graph below).

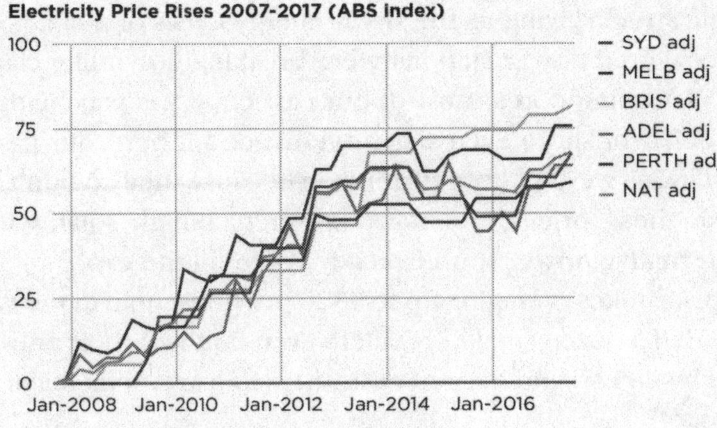

Source: ACCC © Commonwealth of Australia

The main reason was political bungling: governments over-spent on new poles and wires to 'gold-plate' our electricity networks at the expense of people like you and me, then the cost of generating power skyrocketed because of a decade of bickering about carbon taxes, trading schemes and coal industry jobs.

In 2017, according to one leading energy economist, South Australians even had the world's highest electricity prices!

Australians pay highest power prices in world

Exclusive

Ben Potter and Andrew Tillett

Australian residential customers are paying the highest electricity prices in the world – two to three times more than American households – but experts say they need more than information to navigate the thicket of discounts and offers.

South Australian households are paying the highest prices in the world at 47.13¢ per kilowatt hour, more than Germany, Denma...

Electric shock

Retail electricity prices of NEM states, including taxes, compared to selected countries (¢ per kWh)

Region	¢ per kWh
South Australia	47.13
Denmark	44.78
Germany	43.29
Italy	40.30
New South Wales	39.10
Ireland	35.82
Queensland	35.69
Portugal	35.07
Victoria	34.66
	32.84

Prices started to come back to earth after 2017, and then a global pandemic struck, giving us the Great Energy Crisis of 2022.

Our coal-fired power stations were breaking down like clapped-out old VL Commodores, most of our east coast gas was being sold for top dollar offshore even when we needed it here, our gas-fired power stations weren't even turning on because they couldn't make money at those prices, and there weren't enough solar, wind or other alternative power sources ready yet to fill the gap.

Cue price hikes averaging up to $520 per household in the winter of 2022. Half a dozen smaller retailers even doubled their rates (one went up by 285%!) and begged customers to leave. Some have since gone broke.

Small Victorian energy provider says 'only the lazy or crazy would stay' with them

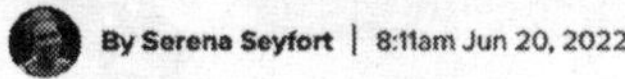
By Serena Seyfort | 8:11am Jun 20, 2022

The upshot: if you didn't switch providers after the winter price hikes of 2022, it's possible you're now paying $1000 more than you have to. That's money that belongs in YOUR pocket and it's easy to put it there.

And that's why we're here – to see if there's any easy money you can save on your power bills.

So once again, let's start with the easiest options and move onto the trickier ones. You choose how many you want to try based on how much time and energy you have to give to it.

In a nutshell

Potential saving	Anywhere from $50 up to $1000 for an average household
Easiest	'Switching' and 'Government rebates'
Next-easiest	'Going solar' (if you own your home) and cutting down your usage
Top tools	OneBigSwitch.com.au, EnergyMadeEasy.gov.au, Compare.energy.vic.gov.au and Energy.gov.au
If I could tell you one thing about energy bills it would be:	Switchers get the best deals!

SWITCHING

Potential saving: Up to $1000 for an average home

If you're in South-east Qld, NSW, Victoria, SA, Tassie or the ACT, you can switch providers to try to save hundreds and sometimes even $1000+ a year. It takes less than 10 minutes and there's no interruption to your power supply, making it my #1 EASIEST way to save on electricity and gas. Here's how:

1. **Grab your last bill.** It should tell you how much electricity you used over the most recent quarter or month, the rates you're paying and any discounts you're getting.
2. **Check the publicly-available plans at the government website EnergyMadeEasy.gov.au (or Compare.energy.vic.gov.au in Victoria).** If your last bill is a PDF email bill, you might be able to just upload it and the website will read it for you and find the cheapest deals. If not, enter your details manually. See which offers they recommend as the cheapest.
3. **If you're a solar customer,** the government sites just don't cut it. You should visit the best of the commercial comparison sites, Wattever.com.au, which also specializes in solar and compares all providers. This is also the easiest site to visit if you're in WA, where it's possible to switch gas providers but not electricity providers.
4. **This next step is optional,** but it's necessary if you also want to check the cheapest Under-the-Table deals. For those, you can check discount clubs such as OneBigSwitch.com.au (where I work), some motoring clubs (e.g. NRMA, RACV, RAA) that negotiate special deals for their members, or loyalty programs at the bank or telco where you're a customer.
5. **You've now got multiple super-cheap offers in your hot little hand.** You're armed and dangerous. At this point, you have a choice: you can pick a winner and switch, or you can call your provider and ask if they can beat those deals. (If you choose to

switch, they'll probably call you anyway and try to make you an offer you can't refuse.) Here's that basic script again:

'Hi there, my name is [Robert De Niro/Insert Your Name Here]. Can you please put me through to someone on your retention team? I've been a loyal customer of yours for _______ years and I'd like to stay on, but I've just received a really good offer from another provider and I think it might be a better deal than the one I'm on. _______ has offered me _______. I wondered whether you can beat it? If you can, I'll lock it in right now.'

6. **Once you decide whether to stay or switch, it will take about five minutes to fill out the form or complete the process over the phone.** You'll be amazed by how easy it is. (Got gas? You can repeat the process above or just take the gas offer that comes with your electricity deal if it looks up to scratch.)

Your supply won't be disconnected when you switch providers – it's just the biller that changes. About the worst thing that can happen is that two retailers end up in a fight over who 'owns' your account.

Your retailer 'owns your meter', as the lingo in the industry goes. When you switch, a new retailer takes over that 'ownership'. If you have a smart meter (like most Victorians do), that changeover can happen straight away, with a ten-day cooling-off period.

If it's not a smart meter (like most people in the rest of Australia), your account can either switch over in 48 hours on the basis of an estimated meter read, or wait for your next scheduled meter read (which is usually once every quarter).

This is one shop where everyone is selling more or less the same thing; the only differences are how they price it, how they deal with their customers and where they source it. A well-known brand does *not* have more reliable electricity than an unknown brand: they might have a better smartphone app or more people in their call centre, but the electrons they sell are the same, so don't be afraid to give a smaller brand a go.

NUMBER CRUNCH

Around 2 million Aussie households switch electricity providers each year. When prices spiked in winter 2022, we broke our record for switching as 452,000 homes moved in just two months. That's over 300 every hour!

True Story: My Dad Switched And Saved $1500 On His Power Bill

After 40 years of feeling like I didn't listen enough to his pearls of wisdom, my dad finally got his revenge.

On TV and in the newspapers, I'd been banging on for a few years now about shopping around and switching energy providers to maximise your discount.

I assumed he'd been listening, but when I asked him to send me his bill, lo and behold he was on a gargantuan, world-beating, jaw-dropping discount of . . . zero!

Dad lives down the coast from Sydney, on a big block in the bush with no gas, and his electricity bill was a whopper – about $1700 a quarter.

But like about 1 in 10 Australians, he hadn't recently shopped around or asked his provider for a better discount. He didn't think he was able to switch in the area where he lived. So he was paying top dollar.

This is not unusual – after all, until the last 20 years or so switching was not possible. Most of us had only one option – the local government-owned supplier (which is still the case for West Australians, the NT and North Queenslanders).

Switching only started when power companies were privatised and pricing was deregulated to make them compete against one another. About a million Australians have still never switched.

So we upgraded my dad to a 28% discount for 12 months with the same provider (he didn't even have to switch in this case), and he saved an estimated $1500 over the next year.

Then he installed solar and now he's laughing.

Too EASY!

TWO POWERFUL *NEW* WAYS TO KNOW IF THERE'S A BETTER DEAL OUT THERE

Until a few years ago, you needed a Nobel Prize in economics to compare electricity plans. Provider A might have been offering a 30% discount and Provider B a 20% discount, but those discounts were off completely different rates, so sometimes the 20% discount worked out cheaper! It was bonkers.

So, in 2019, the federal government introduced a new benchmark 'fair price' for ALL providers to measure their discounts off. Because governments are incapable of ever making anything as simple as it should be, they gave it multiple names that all mean basically the same thing. It's mostly called:

- The 'default market offer', or
- The 'government reference price'.

So really, it's never been easier to find the cheapest deal, because all discount offers now have to be compared to that 'reference price', so you can finally make apples-for-apples comparisons.

It also acts as a quasi-safety net. People who do nothing to shop around for a cheaper electricity plan should be automatically put onto the 'default offer' or 'reference price' so they don't get ripped off too severely. If not, they can demand to be moved to a 'standing offer' equal to the government price.

You still need to shop around to maximise your savings. 80–90% of the deals out there are still cheaper than these new 'default offers', and the best offers available to Price-Chasers are hundreds of dollars cheaper.

Also, bear in mind that the pricing on most plans changes every year at least once. So to maximise your savings you *must* actively switch – or at least upgrade with the same provider – every year or two.

The second powerful new tool is called 'better offer messaging'. This is where your retailer MUST say on your power bill if they have a plan that would be cheaper for you. It doesn't tell you if there are even cheaper rates elsewhere, but it does at least confirm whether you're getting your provider's best current deal.

This is already mandatory in Victoria but it's due to land in NSW, QLD, SA, Tassie and the ACT in the first half of 2023 – so keep an eye out on your next bill.

Insider Trick: The De Niro

Like Robert De Niro's bank-robber character in the movie *Heat*, you gotta at least be *prepared* to walk away if you want access to the best energy deals.

In the energy market, loyalty has gone the way of the dodo – it's as dead as most of the characters by the end of *Heat*.

Loyalty schemes or rewards programs are more common in insurance and groceries and other household bills, and a few of them are worthwhile participating in.

But they're less common in the energy market and I can't think of a single reward I've seen for staying with your provider of electricity and gas that would justify paying a higher rate, so focus on the price first and foremost.

In fact, it's generally the opposite – perversely, the best deals are offered *only* to new customers or to customers who have one foot out the door, De Niro-style.

Don't believe me? Then take the word of the regulator, the Australian Energy Market Commission, who said this:

> ***'Consumers tend to only get a better deal if they leave or threaten to leave a retailer.'***

Many retailers will also move you to a dud plan if you move house or your discount expires – it's up to you to ask for a better one.

About half of new energy plans are taken up by movers, but movers often pay top dollar because who has the time and head-space for checking prices and rates when you're moving house?

This even happened to us one time when we moved house – they put us on a zero-discount plan. I then called up and went from no discount to 28% off in a single phone call. Why? Because I let them know I was prepared to walk, of course.

True Story: Peter From SA Moves House, Then Saves $2000 By Switching

A lot of movers just want to make sure the lights come on and don't have the time or energy to ensure their deal is a good one.

Power companies know this, so they sometimes sell their most expensive offers to movers – often through third parties such as real estate agents and mortgage brokers.

So it was for Peter from the Barossa Valley in South Australia (that's him above), who moved house and agreed to let his real estate agent organise an energy deal for him. Bad idea.

'The first two bills were outrageous, totalling just under $4000 for six months!' he told us. 'When I complained to them, they didn't want to know even though I threatened to change. So I moved.'

The agent had put him on a zero-discount 'standing offer', probably pocketing a commission for doing so, and Peter ended up paying top dollar every time he switched on the telly or the lights.

Over the next six months, thanks to a large new pay-on-time discount, Peter's bills added up to less than half of that initial amount. He saved over $2000.

'This is such a huge difference,' he told me. 'I'm so happy I changed.'

Insider Trick: The Under-the-Table Deal

Most power companies have offers they never show to the general public. These can be significantly better than their best publicly advertised discount.

If you want the cheapest electricity going, it's often going to be on one of these Under-the-Table deals.

They might offer these deals to a special partner that has a large audience (like One Big Switch, or a footy club, or a motoring club, or a bank), or they might offer them to their staff, or they might offer them as 'retention deals' to someone who is leaving. But they don't usually broadcast them to the world. You have to ask.

The key to getting access to these deals is leverage – and you can get that by being a member of one of the groups I've listed above.

If you get access to one of these deals and your current provider tries to match it or beat it, you can end up in a 'Dutch auction' between two providers, and that's when you know you can't lose.

In that situation, you're almost certain to walk away with an absolute killer deal, whichever retailer you choose.

True Story: Melinda Saves $588 A Year By Switching To An Under-The-Table Deal

In my day job over the past eleven years, I've seen hundreds of people save big bucks using Under-the-Table energy deals.

From time to time we go out and meet them, and those are my favourite days in (or out of) the office because it reminds us why we go to work each day.

One of the loveliest families I've met was Melinda and her two daughters Grace and Indii-Annah in Sydney's south-west.

The family needs to use a lot of power to maintain a certain temperature range in their home because of Indii's disability, so there wasn't much more they could do to reduce their usage.

But there were much bigger discounts available than they were getting and, based on analysis of their old bills, we estimated they saved $588 a year by switching to a group-discounted deal we had negotiated.

'We switched from Dodo to a 30% discount with Alinta . . . and you could easily see the savings straight away,' Melinda said. 'It was super easy . . . it took about five minutes and I was done. The savings, as you can see, are ridiculous.'

GOVERNMENT REBATES & CONCESSIONS

Potential saving: Up to $1600

There are hundreds and sometimes even thousands of dollars in energy rebates and concessions available from state and federal governments.

The only problem is, they differ from state to state and change often - so it's hard to summarise in a book like this.

Some states (such as NSW) have much better websites than others (I'm looking at you, SA) to explain what's available.

The best central place to search for them is the federal government website Energy.gov.au - where you'll find rebates and concessions for two broad categories of people:

Category 1 – Pensioners, concession card holders and low-income households:

Most states have energy rebates or cost of living rebates for you. In some cases, you need to make sure your energy retailer has your concession card number and it should be applied automatically. In others, the state government pays you an annual sum to help with a range of bills.

As I said, they do change often but examples of rebates in 2022 included:

- $395 p.a. in NSW
- 17.5% of electricity and gas bills in VIC
- $414 in QLD
- $682 for energy and cost of living in SA
- $310 in WA
- $1000 in the ACT
- $513 in TAS
- $465 in the NT

Some states also have rebates for low-income households or self-funded retirees who hold a Commonwealth Seniors Health Card (these are income-tested NOT asset-tested so check your availability). In NSW, there's also a rebate for those who receive the Family Tax Benefit and in QLD there's some help for asylum seekers. In SA there's also a range of Centrelink payments that qualify you for rebates.

NSW and QLD also have up to $1600 in vouchers available to households experiencing a financial emergency.

I keep an updated list on the One Big Switch website, or check the Energy.gov.au site above for the latest.

Category 2 – Those who want to make their homes more energy efficient:
Most governments have targets for energy efficiency and some will even pay households to help achieve them.

Before you spend a cent upgrading your appliances or installing solar or batteries, just check if there's some government help available. Here are just a few recent examples at the time of writing:

NSW offered about $30 per globe for households that replace old light globes with LEDs, and up to $4000 for low-income households that install solar or other energy-efficient appliances.

The ACT offered interest-free loans up to $15,000 for homes to install solar panels, batteries and other energy-efficient appliances.

Victoria's Energy Upgrades program offers households up to $6600 back for upgrading to new energy-efficient appliances, and $2400 in rebates for solar installations.

Most states also offer rebates of $3000–$3500 for new electric vehicles.

GO SOLAR (IF YOU CAN)

Potential saving: Up to 90% of your power bills
We're breaking records in this area too: almost every year, Aussies install a record amount of new solar power on our rooftops.

We have more panels per head of capita than any country in the world.

When power prices skyrocketed in 2022 and headlines screamed about the latest 'ENERGY PRICE CRISIS', those who were lucky enough to have a roof-full of panels just shrugged and got on with their daily lives.

It's desperately unfair on people who can't go solar, of course – if you're a renter or (often) if you live in an apartment, solar power might not be an option for you.

But fortunately, having thousands of dollars in cash savings is no longer an entry requirement.

An average-sized system could cost anywhere from $4000–$10,000, but there are now multiple ways to pay for solar without putting down a single dollar upfront, so check out these options for starters:

- **Green loans** with rates below 10% p.a. (providers include CBA, Brighte, Plenti and Bank Australia)
- **Zero-interest Buy Now Pay Later schemes** (Brighte also offers these, as do many installers – note that because they're not making any interest, the price will not be as cheap as other options)
- **'Power purchase agreements'** where you pay a fixed cost of say $120 per month for 10 years and you get panels and a battery which you own outright at the end of the payment period (providers include ShineHub and EnergyAustralia)

If you pay upfront, the average 'payback time' for a solar system is now around 4–6 years, depending on your usage and the size of the system.

But you might also be able to use the finance options above to effectively lower your energy costs from day one – for example, if you have a $200/month power bill and you sign up for a $120/month power purchase agreement that lowers your power bill by 80%, you'll be spending less overall on electricity from the get-go while you pay off the plan over 10 years.

A word of warning, though: every home is different. Some of us are home all day and can use all the energy our solar panels generate. Others are only home at night and might need a battery to store it. Some of us have electric cars and might want a bigger system to charge them; others have swimming pools and might want to use solar power to heat them.

There's no one-size-fits-all rule: you need to get a system designed for your particular home and maybe an energy audit first to see how you're using your electricity and gas (some councils offer these or subsidise them).

Use this checklist to avoid the SOLAR COWBOYS and SHONKS!

Panels

☑ These should be ranked 'Tier 1' by Bloomberg New Energy Finance, which indicates a financially-stable manufacturer.

☑ Their power output should be around 300W (the older ones were 250W).

☑ They should be 'mono PERC half-cut' – the most popular type at the moment.

☑ Demand a 25-year performance warranty and a 12 or 15-year product warranty.

Inverter

☑ This is even more important than the panels, because it's the most likely element to fail in the first 10 years.

☑ If you're on a limited budget, prioritise a premium inverter over premium panels.

☑ European inverters cost about $1000–$1200 more, as a rule.

☑ Look for a 5-year warranty – or even better, 10 years – on a reputable brand. Sometimes you can pay to extend a warranty to 10 years.

Batteries

☑ At $8000-plus, they're not for everyone, but they are coming down in price.

☑ Lithium Iron Phosphate batteries have warranties of 80% of original capacity after 10 years (where other battery chemistries only have 60% or 70% guarantees after 10 years). Lithium Iron Phosphate batteries can also be re-charged around 8,000–10,000 times, where other battery chemistries can only take around 4,000–6,000 recharges.

☑ They're more likely to suit you if you use most of your energy at night, and if you connect up to a 'Virtual Power Plant' – or if you want to charge an electric vehicle perhaps.

Retailer and Installer

☑ Look for the 1100-plus retailers that are 'Clean Energy Council-approved', which means they've agreed to meet higher standards than the bare minimum required by government.

☑ For installers, ask if they're 'Clean Energy Council accredited' (not just a CEC member).

☑ Look for a warranty on installation of at least 5 years, if not 10 - and the longer a company has been around for, the better.

Energy monitoring

☑ Does the package include energy monitoring? This is an app that shows you how much energy your system is producing and where it's going. It's important because it's the only way you'll know if your system is working properly.

☑ It also shows the retailer is committing to making your system work long-term. Some companies don't want to know about you anymore once they've installed the hardware.

Price!

☑ There is such a thing as 'too cheap' when it comes to solar. Solar products are not like electricity, where everyone is basically selling the same thing; some hardware is better than others, as are some installers. Very cheap solar deals can be a sign of cutting corners. So you're looking for that sweet spot where the price is good but you're also getting maximum value for your buck.

☑ 6.5 or 6.6kW is the most common system size for a typical family, which should cost around $3000–$6000 including government rebates. The difference between $3000 and $6000 will often be whether the panels and inverter are European-made. Just like cars, they cost more but they may not be necessary. Toyotas are good cars, and many Chinese brands make good solar panels.

☑ Don't get too hung up on 'payback time'. A typical household can take out finance to fund solar and spend less than they used to spend on grid electricity - so they're saving from day one.

(Sources: Alex Georgiou at ShineHub and Finn Peacock's 'Good Solar Guide')

THE BIG ENERGY-GUZZLERS

Potential saving: Hundreds or even thousands of dollars

If you've done all you can to ensure your plan is cheap, or if you're in a state where you can't switch, the only other option for saving on power bills is to *use less*!

Start by concentrating on the Big Three Energy-Guzzlers: heating/cooling, hot water and pools.

Heating & Cooling

Save up to $5300 over 12 years by choosing an energy-efficient appliance. That's how much cheaper it is to run a heat pump reverse-cycle air conditioner than a gas heater nowadays – plus it cools you down in summer if need be. So buying the right hardware is the #1 way to save big over time. The difference in running costs gets bigger and bigger the more solar electricity you use to power heating and cooling.

Dial the heater down. There's research that shows men are most comfortable at about 22 degrees and women at about 24 degrees. So don't start at 25 degrees in winter as it may be unnecessary, especially if the house is full of blokes! Start low, see if it's comfortable, and only go hotter if you need to.

> **NUMBER CRUNCH**
>
> Every degree of temperature on the thermostat can add about $100 over the season.

Dial the air con up! Same principle. When cooling your home down, start with a higher target temperature such as 24 degrees first and see if it's comfortable before blasting out the icy-cold air.

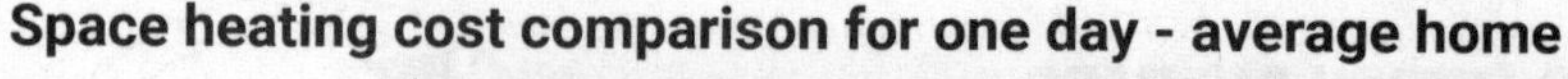

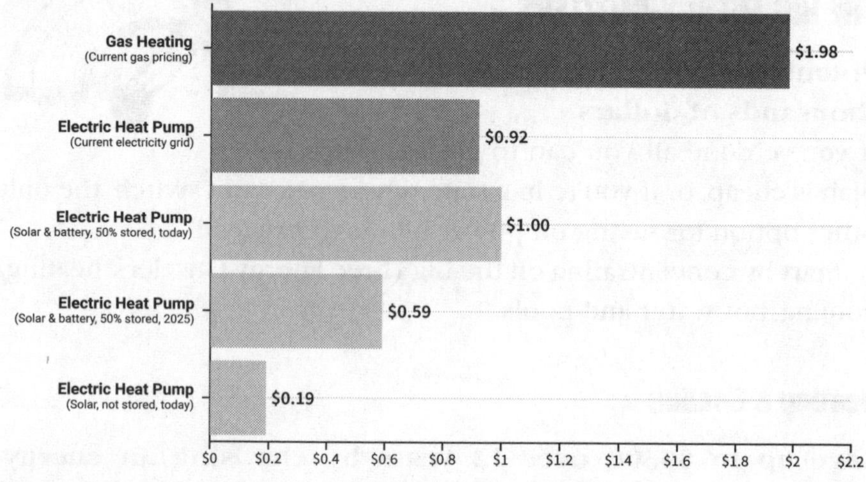

Source: © Rewiring Australia – The Big Switch – Saul Griffith

Dial the hot water down too. Most hot water systems have a thermostat too and it costs a lot more to heat your hot water to 70 degrees than it does to 50 degrees.

Avoid bar heaters and fan heaters if you can. Reverse-cycle air conditioners, for example, are at least 2.5 times more efficient.

Only heat or cool the rooms you are using, rather than the whole house. Close the doors and insulate the room you're in. Cuddle each other!

Put a jumper on, as my mother used to say! Dress for the season and you won't need as much heating or cooling in the first place.

Hot Water

Save up to $2800 over 12 years by choosing an energy-efficient appliance. That's how much cheaper it is to run a heat pump hot water system than a gas system – even though instantaneous gas hot water used to be cheaper. Again, the difference in running costs gets bigger and bigger if you have solar.

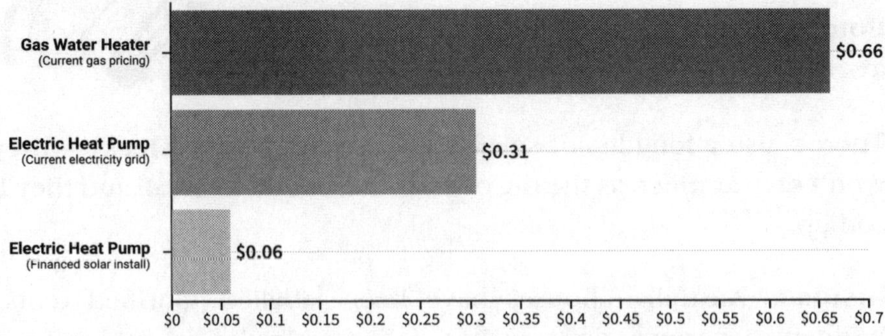

Source: © Rewiring Australia – The Big Switch – Saul Griffith

Take shorter showers. Did you know showering can make up to 60% of your hot water usage?

A shower uses less energy than a bath – especially if you shower in twos!

Pools & Spas

Run the pool or spa pump at night on an off-peak tariff or controlled load meter to minimise the cost.A pool pump can cost anywhere from $600 to $1500 a year to run and a spa costs about $240.

BUT if you have solar, run it during the day when your electricity is free.

Clean pool filters often to maximise your pump's efficiency.

Cover it up. An insulated cover on pools and spas will save money.

Again, solar is far cheaper than gas or mains electricity for heating pools.

Fill it in or cover it over if you never use it. I've seen some great decks built over pools – if someone wants the pool back in future, it's still there 'below deck'.

THE SMALLER SUCKERS

Potential saving: $100–$200 on average

There's also a long list of smaller efficiencies you can make – they won't save as much as the big ones above but do them all and they'll add up.

Insulate. Australian houses have been labelled 'glorified tents'. Window coverings, door snakes and double-glazing can make a big difference over time. Insulation of any kind is hugely helpful in keeping a consistent temperature.

Avoid 'vampire power'. This is the power that unused appliances can 'suck' from your power points. You can save about 10% by turning appliances off at the power point when not using them. On one of my bills, it even added up to over 15% of my usage!

Your estimated energy use by appliance category

We estimate that 16% of your usage went towards standby and always on.*

Category	Cost
Cooking	$20
Standby and always on	$15
Home entertainment	$14
Fridges & freezers	$12
Lighting	$12
Laundry & dishwasher	$9
Anything else	$9

Switch off the beer fridge. They tend to be older appliances, half-full and therefore less energy efficient, and can chew through more than $250 a year. So just turn the beer fridge off in between times and turn it back on a few hours before your big event, or fill an esky with ice instead!

Stars matter. A three-star fridge/freezer can be $900 cheaper than a one-star appliance over the life of the machine. This is also a good reason to consider upgrading appliances sometimes, even if there's an initial cost to buy a new one.

Use timers to control heating and cooling. Don't be slack: turn off appliances if you don't need them.

Keep your oven serviced. Keep the seals tight and the oven clean to ensure no heat is wasted.

Clean the filters on the rangehood regularly. Vent the exhaust to outside your home and use the exhaust fan on the lowest speed.

Stack the dishwasher and don't run it until it's completely full. Same with the washing machine. Use cold water where possible.

Electric fan-type ovens are more efficient than conventional ovens.

Shift your usage. If you're on a plan that has off-peak or 'controlled load' rates, you can save about $260 a year by moving your washing machine, dishwasher or water heater to off-peak rates. Turn them on when you go to bed.

BUT use your appliances during the day instead if you have solar power, so that they run for free.

Spin dry before hanging out a load of washing, rather than using the dryer for the whole job.

Clean the dryer's lint filter regularly. Or ditch the dryer altogether if you live in a dry part of the country. It may take a little longer but it sure saves a lot of money.

Switch off lights in those rooms that aren't being used. It may seem a very obvious move but as any parent will attest, it's a constant battle!

Opt for energy-efficient lightbulbs – try longer-lasting LED globes. Some of these bulbs are also dimmable and some state governments will pay you to install them.

DOES GREENPOWER COST MORE?

Accredited GreenPower costs a bit more – up to about $100–$200 a year for a typical home – but not as much as most people probably assume.

Most retailers will now give you the option of saying that you want say 25%, 50% or 100% of your power to be green.

This doesn't mean the energy you use is actually from solar or wind or hydro sources – once the power goes into the grid it's all mixed together into a big electricity soup – but it does mean your retailer will ensure they buy the equivalent amount of power from green sources. Some retailers are also carbon-neutral, which means that they buy carbon credits to offset their emissions – but not necessarily that they buy more GreenPower.

INSIDE INFO

Thanks to some dopey red tape, only renewable power sources that were added to the grid since the legislation was enacted in the 1990s can be accredited as official 'GreenPower', so some of the older hydro-electric schemes such as Tasmania's system do not qualify – even though they're every bit as renewable as the newer ones. This disadvantages some retailers, such as Momentum Energy, who get their power from these older schemes.

Greenpeace produces a 'Green Electricity Guide' ranking the various retailers according to six criteria:

- Providing clean, renewable energy
- Ending coal use by 2030
- Halting fossil fuel expansion
- Support for new renewable energy
- Transparency of marketing
- Pollution and environmental harm

In 2022, Diamond Energy came out on top with 5 stars, followed by Momentum, Energy Locals and Indigo Power (all 4.5 stars).

The 'Big Three' – AGL, Origin and EnergyAustralia – all got one star each.

Coming soon to Australian power bills (but so is Christmas): 'automated switching' and 'open data'

If you just wish someone else would do it all for you, that day is approaching (albeit slowly).

A number of businesses are already experimenting with 'do-it-for-me' energy switching services: you pay them a fee and they notify you every time they think they can save you say $50 or $100 by switching.

CHOICE launched one of these services but abandoned it after a year. One Big Switch even dabbled with it at one point.And there's a mob called Bill Hero who are still trying to make it work.

It's been slow progress, but perhaps government reforms could accelerate this when power bills become part of the new 'open data' rules that will also apply to banking and telco bills.

The basic idea is that you'll be able to request for your energy bill data to be securely shared with a comparison service or energy retailer with the push of a button.

They will then be able to tell you exactly how much you could save by switching – and which deal is best for you.

But don't hold your breath: this revolution has been 'just around the corner' for the past decade – ever since I've been involved in helping people to save money on power bills. So I'll believe it when I see it . . .

In the meantime, let's stick with the tried and tested ways to save that I've outlined here.

Insider Trick: The Squeaky Wheel

Been overcharged by your energy retailer? Unfairly disconnected? Bullied by a pushy door-to-door salesperson?

More than 100,000 households around the country report a problem with their retailer each year. That's 2000 a week, or almost 300 of us every day!

So if you need to complain about a power provider you'll have plenty of company, and there are some well-organised systems in place to help you.

(NB: If the complaint relates to a problem with your meter, an outage or other supply issue, you actually need to contact your energy distributor – that's the company that owns the poles and wires that bring the power to your home. How do I know who my bloody distributor is, I hear you ask? Good question! You can check your bill, ask your retailer (who sends you the bill), or look for more info here: www.aer.gov.au/consumers/making-a-complaint/who-is-my-distributor)

For complaints to do with your *retailer*, the best approach is to follow the 'Squeaky Wheel' strategy I explained in Part 2:

STEP #1:

Contact the retailer. Tell them (*politely but firmly!*) what the problem is and what you want them to do to fix it. If they don't agree, ask to speak to a manager and tell them the same thing.

Write down their name, the time of the call or email, and their response. Ask for their email address so you can put your complaint and your request in writing to them, to ensure they have a record of it. Write down a reference number too, if they provide one. Write once, call once.

If you still don't get a resolution . . .

STEP #2:

Take it public. Post a (*polite but firm, remember!*) comment on their Twitter and Facebook pages. Wait 24 hours.

If you *still* don't get a resolution . . .

STEP #3:

Make it official. Contact the energy ombudsman in your state or territory and dob on them!

It's a free service and they'll try to resolve your issue. Best of all, they'll make your retailer take you seriously:

NSW Energy & Water Ombudsman:
www.ewon.com.au/

Energy & Water Ombudsman Victoria:
www.ewov.com.au/

Energy & Water Ombudsman Queensland:
www.ewoq.com.au/

Energy & Water Ombudsman SA:
www.ewosa.com.au/

Energy & Water Ombudsman WA:
www.ombudsman.wa.gov.au/energyandwater/

Energy Ombudsman Tasmania:
www.energyombudsman.tas.gov.au/

Energy Ombudsman ACT:
www.acat.act.gov.au/

What if I can't pay my bill?

Every retailer must have a 'hardship program' for people in your situation. Ask them about it. It will make it possible for you to negotiate a payment plan with the retailer. They're not supposed to just cut you off, but you need to ask to be put on this program to avoid disconnection, so do speak up!

CHAPTER 15
TELCO

> 'I love money. I love everything about it. I bought some pretty good stuff. Got me a $300 pair of socks. Got a fur sink. An electric dog polisher. A gasoline powered turtleneck sweater. And, of course, I bought some dumb stuff, too.'
> **Steve Martin**

There might be some easy money on offer here for more Australians than in any other household bill. The reason is that half of us are with the nation's most expensive provider.

If you're an average Telstra customer, you can probably save around $500 a year in minutes by switching your internet and mobile(s) to a cheaper telco.

Take a deep breath. The sky won't fall in. Ask the other half of the population how their internet speeds and mobile reception are and you'll find that in most cases, they're just fine thanks.

I think I understand why so many people remain with the Big T. There's a reason they call energy and telco 'utilities' – they're pretty bloody useful, some might even say indispensable. We just need them to work.

But the idea that Telstra always works better is like the idea that Qantas is the greatest airline on earth: they're both myths. As I write this, Telstra is the 5th fastest NBN provider in the country, according to the latest ACCC research – so why are its customers paying more?

(If you're still grappling with this one, read 'To Telstra, or not to Telstra' below for more of the pros and cons.)

Whichever camp you're in, your telco bill is probably one of the easiest of the lot to compare online, thanks to the new super-powers bestowed on us by the internet.

The only tough bit is deciding what data limits and speeds and features you need. Once you've answered those questions, searching and saving hundreds can be a cinch.

It's also one of the easiest bills to switch. You can take your mobile number with you when you move providers, and switch your broadband in a matter of minutes.

So let's see if there's some easy money out there for you, without sacrificing speed or reception. Once again, we'll start with the easiest of the easy.

In a nutshell

Potential saving	Anywhere from $50 up to $1000 for an average household
Easiest	'Switching providers' and 'Cutting landlines'
Next-easiest	'Right-sizing your plan' and 'Speed-testing'
Top tools	WhistleOut.com.au is hands-down the best telco comparison website. There's no government equivalent.
If I could tell you one thing about telco bills it would be:	These products are the classic moving target. Switch annually and you'll get more for less.

SWITCHING

Potential saving: Up to $1000 for an average home

It's never been easier to save between $50 and $1000 p.a. on your telco bills in 20 minutes or less. Here's a brief guide to notching up a quick result:

1. **Check your current mobile or broadband plan:** What do you pay each month? What's your data download limit? Which network is it on (if it's mobile)? What's the speed (if it's NBN)? What else is included? (Calls? Phone? Modem?) Do you want the same things from a new plan?
2. **Go to WhistleOut.com.au, Australia's most comprehensive telco comparison site.** These guys are total telco nerds. Enter the info about what you're looking for – limits, speeds, hardware and other inclusions. (Don't know what you need? In that case, read the rest of this chapter and then come back to this part.)
3. **See which plans they recommend.** They might show a couple of 'featured' ones first who pay for the top spot, but then they'll rank the rest from cheapest to most expensive. Most of the cheap ones will be brands you've hardly heard of. Most of the expensive ones you'll know. Ask yourself: does the brand matter? Their mobile network or their NBN 'pipes' are the same as the big guys. The only difference will be the price, the customer service, and maybe the hardware they include. Your call. (I often go for brands in the middle somewhere – established enough to know their stuff but new enough to be hungry for customers.)
4. **At this point, if you're happy to switch and you don't like haggling, you can just sign up to the plan you've picked.** But if you like your current provider, call them up and tell them about the plan you're thinking of moving to. Ask them to beat it. Telcos are super-competitive and they'll probably play ball. Here's that basic script again:

'Hi there, my name is [Robert De Niro/Insert Your Name Here]. Perhaps you could put me through to someone on your retention team to see if they can help? I've been a loyal customer of yours for _______ years and I'd like to stay on, but I've just received a really good offer from another provider and I think it might be a better deal than the one I'm on. _______ has offered me _______ . I wondered whether you can match it or even beat it? If you can, I'll lock it in right now.'

INSIDE INFO

There are only three mobile networks in Australia (Telstra, Optus and Vodafone). Every mobile plan is on one of those three! So it's possible to get a mobile plan on the Telstra network that costs less than the equivalent Telstra plan, and the same applies to Optus and Vodafone.

In fact, many smaller providers are even owned by the Big Three: Telstra owns Belong; Optus owns amaysim, Gomo and Vaya; and Vodafone owns TPG, iiNet and Felix.

If you're in a well-serviced area, there may be no good reason to pay extra for a big name. Have a look at some of the brands below that operate on the big-name networks:

Telstra 4G network	Optus 4G network	Vodafone 4G network
Aldi Mobile	amaysim	Felix
Belong	Catch Connect	Kogan Mobile
Boost Mobile	Coles Mobile	Lebara Mobile
Lycamobile	Dodo	Internode
Pennytel	Southern Phone	TPG
Mate	Aussie Broadband	iiNet
Exetel	Gomo	

Telechoice	Southern Phone	
Think Mobile	Moose Mobile	
Woolworths Mobile	Spintel	
Nu Mobile	Vaya	

Insider Trick: The Moving Target

Telco plans are the biggest moving target of the lot!

They change faster than any other major household bill, because they're based on new technology – and technology in this area is advancing at warp speed.

Look at it this way. In 2010, Aussies downloaded about 250,000 terabytes of data on our broadband plans. By 2021, that had skyrocketed to 10.2 million terabytes!

That's a 4080% increase, or *40.8 times* as many songs, movies, *Game of Thrones* episodes, YouTube cat videos, Google searches, spreadsheets, emails, pouty Instagram selfies and TikTok dances as 11 years before!

Fortunately, our data plans haven't become 40.8 times more expensive, and that's because the technology is moving fast enough to keep up with our data obsession: in other words, data is becoming cheaper for the telcos to move, so they're able to give us more and more for about the same price.

Have you ever been offered a free upgrade to your data limit? You should have been. Telco is one of the only industries where providers do sometimes give you more for the same price, but don't wait for the phone to ring. Check in once every year or two to see what the new 'going rate' is.

Insider Trick: The Elizabeth Taylor

This trick is about taking honeymoon offer after honeymoon offer, and never paying the Sleeping Beauty price.

Because the telco market moves faster than Australia changes prime ministers, it pays to check in whenever your contract expires and see what's available now.

If you've been married to your telco on a contract for a year or two, the telco dating scene will probably look quite different. You'll be like a middle-aged divorcee discovering Tinder for the first time.

In fact, even contracts are becoming more rare in the telco world, unless you're buying an actual device. Most plans are now month-to-month so you're not tied down.

CUT THE LANDLINE

Potential saving: Up to $600 for an average home

True landlines have gone the way of the dodo as the old copper network was cut off, but many households still pay for a home phone. I like to ask people who have a home phone this question:

"When was the last time it rang with anyone other than the phone company or a scammer on the other end?"

A family friend told me recently that she only ever uses her home phone to call her mobile when she's lost it. I had to chuckle. But really, for most of us this is a redundant technology and an easy saving of up to $600.

As I write this, Telstra sells a home phone plan with unlimited calls within Australia for $55 a month. But there are mobile deals with the same included calls starting at just $10 a month – and you can pick that phone up and take it out with you too!

This has become one of the telcos' greatest rorts. If there's a good reason for you to have one, then fair enough. I won't give you a hard time. Good reasons include:

- 'I have lousy mobile reception.'
- 'It costs me nothing extra. E.g. It's included for free in my internet plan.'
- 'I believe mobiles give you cancer/the Russian government is listening in/[insert other implacable personal opinion].'

But if you *don't* have a good reason, that means you're throwing cash away on a service you don't need. By the way, the following are no longer good reasons:

- 'It's cheaper than a mobile.' Clearly, it's not anymore.
- 'It's expensive to call long distance on mobiles.' Again, not true. Many cheap mobile plans have unlimited national and mobile calls and some have international calls included too.
- 'It's part of a bundle.' But that doesn't make it necessary. Telcos toss things like this into bundles to make you feel like you're getting extra value for paying a higher price, whereas in reality you might be able to dump the landline and put together the services you need from a range of providers and save hundreds.
- 'I don't want to give the number up.' This is understandable but there are ways around it – you can always divert it to a mobile number for six months, for example, while everyone catches up on your move. This will cost less than the landline. Also, refer to my question above re: does anyone ever call it?

RIGHT-SIZING

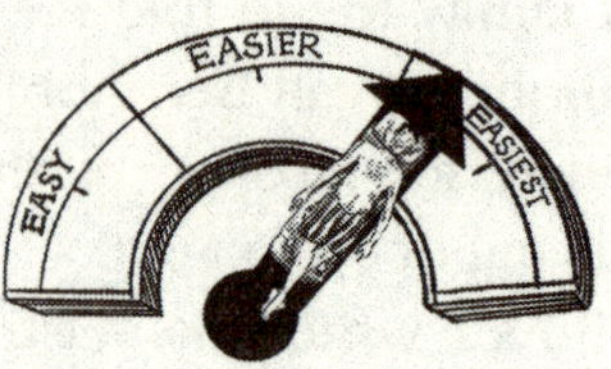

Potential saving: Up to $300 for an average home

There are more mobile phones than people in Australia, and almost every home is now connected to the NBN.

So there are only two ways for telcos to make more money – convince us to switch, or sell us an upgrade.

In recent years, the big telcos have been trying to convince us to move to bigger data plans and faster internet plans.

To some extent, that might be necessary – we're using more data than ever and we need faster and faster wi-fi.

But some of us have been hoodwinked and we're paying for way more data or speed than we can use. So there's some easy money to be saved by 'right-sizing' our plans. Here's how …

Right-Size Your Mobile Plan:

The big telcos occasionally offer plans with as much as 500GB of data per month with a big discount of say $50 off each bill. It looks like a killer deal, but can anyone really use that much data?

NUMBER CRUNCH

If you watched *Stranger Things* in high definition on Netflix on your phone for 16 non-stop hours a day for an entire month, you'd still have trouble chewing through 500GB of data.

In fact, the ACCC says the average Aussie only uses around 15–20GB of mobile data a month. So be realistic and it could save you hundreds of dollars.

Your current mobile provider can tell you how much data you're using: it might be visible in their app or you can just ask them.

Then go to WhistleOut.com.au and search for a plan at the right level.

Australians used to waste over $315 million a year on excess data charges from busting our mobile caps. But you just don't hear as many excess data horror stories as you used to. That's for three reasons:

1. Many telcos no longer charge excess data fees – instead they just slow you down once you bust the cap.
2. Some telcos now offer 'data banking', where unused data from one month rolls over into the next.

3. Providers are also now required to send you mandatory usage notifications when you reach 50%, 85% and 100% of your voice, SMS and data allowance – so you should see it coming.

Right-Size Your Internet Plan:

Since the pandemic, fast NBN plans with speeds of 60Mbps and above have become more popular. For some of us, working from home made it necessary – but for most of us, a standard plan will do the trick.

If you're the internet equivalent of one of those middle-aged men who drive Ferraris at 50kph around the streets of the inner city, maybe you could save a few hundred bucks by parking your ego.

There are several speed options with fixed-line NBN and they've recently re-jigged how they define them:

Product name	Peak hour speed
Basic	At least 13Mbps
Standard	At least 30Mbps
Fast	At least 60Mbps
Super Fast	At least 150Mbps

Are you a one or two person household browsing the internet, sending emails and streaming TV and music in standard definition? Basic plans might be OK, starting from about $50/month.

Three to four person households who also want to stream in HD, download files, play some games and work from home will need at least a Standard plan, from about $60/month.

You'll only need Fast NBN (starting around $70/month) if you want five or more people to be online at the same time, doing all of the above as well as streaming 4K video and downloading large files.

And Super Fast? That's the Ferrari I mentioned earlier. Unless you're actually making video games, you'll probably never know what it's capable of . . .

Once you've picked your speed, you can punch it in at a comparison website such as WhistleOut and move onto picking a provider.

Who's the fastest internet provider?

This changes from time to time, and it depends who you ask, but the good news is there's no longer much difference between the 10 biggest providers.

The ACCC reports on it every three months by monitoring a sample of customers from 10 of the biggest providers. Telstra topped the charts in most of the early tests 5 years ago but they had dropped as low as fifth in 2022. Exetel and Optus were on top.

As you can see from the graph below, 9 out of the 10 providers achieved at least 91% of their advertised speeds during the busiest hour of the day (only MyRepublic flopped, with 75%).

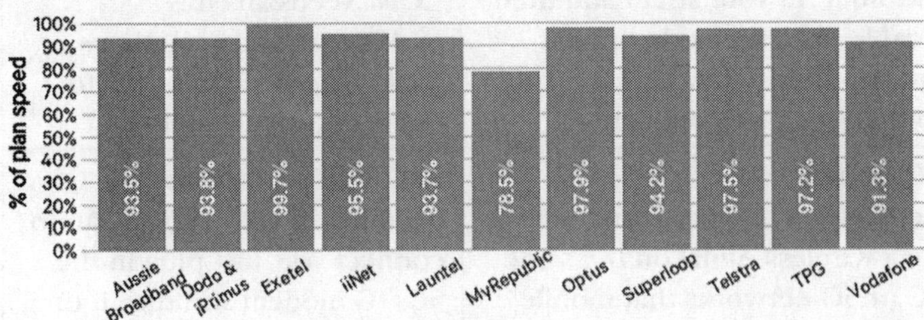

Source: ACCC © Commonwealth of Australia

The Ookla speed test website also publishes rankings from time to time and their most recent ones in 2021 found Aussie Broadband was fastest, then Optus and iiNet. Anyone can use Ookla to see how fast their internet connection is, so these results are based on those who have used the Ookla test online.

Traffic on the road slows down at peak hour, and so too does the internet. Providers now have to advertise an average 'evening speed' or 'speed during busy hours' on their plans, so you can get a more accurate idea of what you'll experience at 8pm when everyone watches the latest *House of the Dragon* episode at the same time.

What about 5G, Cable, ADSL, Satellite and wireless internet?

NBN is now the #1 way to access the internet in Australia but it's not the only way. If you can't get the NBN, or it's no good at your place, or you just want to try something else, there's also 5G, Cable, ADSL, Satellite and wireless internet. They're just different types of 'pipe' that bring the 'Netflix and chill' into your home.

For most homes, the choice is now between NBN and 5G. Here are the pros and cons:

CONNECTION TYPE	PROS & CONS
NBN: Involves running fibre optics to the 'node' in your street and then a cable from the node to your house – unless you have a 'Fibre to the Premises' connection.	PRO: Built to take the majority of the nation's internet traffic. CON: Needs an NBN middleman and sometimes it can take days or weeks to connect or fix a fault.
5G or 4G: No cables! This broadband arrives via a wireless signal on the same 4G or 5G networks that mobile phones use.	PRO: Can be very fast. No need for an NBN technician to connect you. Just plug in the 5G/4G modem and turn it on. CON: Reception depends on your location, just like a mobile phone, and the networks would not cope if everyone connected.

Some more tightarse telco tips:

If you've got a home internet plan, you can now use mobile apps such as WhatsApp or Facebook Messenger to call friends and family anywhere for free.

Telstra is creating a widespread FREE wi-fi network out of thousands of its old payphones for anyone – not just Telstra customers – so make the most of it if there's one nearby.

Whenever you are in a wi-fi network that you have access to, don't use your mobile data. As long as you have wi-fi turned on on your phone, and you've entered the wi-fi password into that phone in the past, it will connect to that network and use wi-fi data not mobile data. So, to give the obvious examples . . . use the wi-fi at work instead of your mobile data. Use the wi-fi at the cafe if they have a free network, too. Use the wi-fi anywhere there's wi-fi that's already paid for!

If you can't afford a Basic NBN plan, or you just don't need it, mobile plans are faster anyhow and some now feature so much data for so little money that you might be better off using them to access the internet. It helps if your plan allows you to 'tether' – this means using your phone as a modem to run other appliances at home such as laptops or desktop computers – and it also helps if certain apps you use a lot, such as streaming apps, are 'unmetered' on your plan, meaning they don't count towards your data limit.

SPEED-TESTING

Potential saving: Up to $300 for an average home

Testing your speed is free and takes two minutes. It won't save you money per se, but if you identify a hardware problem that's slowing your wi-fi down, then fixing it could save you hundreds of dollars over time.

Often, people blame their provider if their internet's too slow. But sometimes it's your modem that's the problem, or where it's located – and fixing that might save you the cost of upgrading to a higher speed tier or a more expensive provider.

Too EASY! You can check your speeds anytime for free using the Ookla Speed Test online at www.speedtest.net/

If your speeds are too slow, try these fixes:

1. **Move the modem/router.** If it's in a cupboard or at one end of the house, the Netflix has to fly through doors and walls and past baby monitors and microwaves using the same radio frequency. So put it in the middle of the house, out in the open, like a bunch of flowers.
2. **Power cycle it!** It's the oldest trick in the book and the secret weapon of IT help desks the world over. We're going to turn everything off, and turn it all on again. When you power cycle your NBN box, modem and router, it clears the memory, gets rid of any old jobs that are bogging them down, and selects the best channel when it starts up again. To do it properly, unplug each device, wait 30 seconds, plug it back in and turn it on. Then, claim full credit.
3. **Switch your wi-fi frequency band.** This sounds technical but it's not really. Most modems' wi-fi networks work on two different frequencies: they're called 2.4 GHz and 5 GHz and that's why you can often see two versions of your wi-fi when you go to connect. So, if you're having trouble when connected to one band, try the other one!

PRO TIP

The 2.4 GHz frequency is like a marathon runner – it's better at travelling long distances but it's a bit slower than the 5 GHz frequency, which is the Usain Bolt of wi-fi – it's faster but over short distances. Ideally, connect these devices to these frequencies to maximise your wi-fi performance:

Best for 2.4 GHz:	Best for 5 GHz:
Smart speakers Smart home devices Security cameras	Gaming consoles PCs Smart TVs

To Telstra, or not to Telstra? That is the question

For better or worse, no other industry has such a massive concentration of customers with one single provider. The former government monopoly was privatised from 1997 onwards and it still has about half of Aussie telco customers. Some need to be with the Big T, but many are Sleeping Beauties with a bad case of loss aversion and status quo bias.

Just leaving Telstra is a way of saving some easy money, so if you're one of the 50%, let's delve a bit deeper into whether you're a candidate for de-Telstrafication.

Here are some reasons for staying with Telstra.

REASON #1:	You live or work in regional Oz, in a spot where there's no other viable mobile network, so of course you're prepared to pay more.
REASON #2:	Your work pays for it.
REASON #3:	You're a horse racing nut who needs Foxtel and your bundle with Telstra works out cheaper than just getting the Foxtel on its own.

These, on the other hand, are not reasons for staying – they're myths.

MYTH #1:	There are valuable extra features such as 5G access, a rewards program and free modem (all of these are either available cheaper or mostly worthless).
MYTH #2:	You've just always been with Telstra and it pays to be loyal.
MYTH #3:	You've got a bundle and it can't be separated. Oh yes it can – that's just what they want you to think.

Telstra's network is indeed better in the bush. All three mobile networks – Telstra, Optus and Vodafone – claim they cover 98% or 99% of Australians but that's the population, not the landmass, and most of us live in the coastal cities. So outside the big smoke, it's often Telstra or nothing at all. But remember that there are other providers that operate on the Telstra network, so you might have some choice after all. Some of them are even owned by Telstra (like Belong, sometimes nicknamed 'Little T').

In the cities, however, there is now very little difference in coverage. Even Vodafone, whose network once saw it nicknamed 'Vodafail', has now built a much better 4G network in metro areas. So mostly it depends where you live and work.

If you want to see what each network is like in your area, you can do so by entering an address at each network's coverage page:

TELSTRA:
www.telstra.com.au/coverage-networks/our-coverage

OPTUS:
www.optus.com.au/shop/mobile/network/coverage

VODAFONE:
www.vodafone.com.au/network/coverage-checker

As for average mobile network speeds, it depends. Opensignal says Optus had the fastest 5G network in 2022. But Ookla measures the speed of all three networks and Telstra is indeed the fastest overall, followed by Optus in a close second and Vodafone a distant third. Here are the mid-2022 results below.

	Speed Score
Telstra	107.25
Optus	102.76
Vodafone	67.81

Source: Ookla

Case Study: Telstra bundle vs my home-made bundle

Not that long ago, if you wanted to watch NRL, AFL and rugby, plus a big family internet plan, a big-data mobile plan and a home phone, you often paid Telstra more than $250 a month for the privilege. (Some people will still be paying these old prices. Last time I checked, Foxtel's Platinum package alone was $140 a month.)

Foxtel now offers broadband and a pay TV + internet bundle will set you back $215/month. The Telstra equivalent starts at $184/month but rises to $235/month.

But by 2022, thanks to the revolution of streaming services, you could get the equivalent of all that for much less.

Let's take a snapshot from mid-2022 and compare an example of a Telstra bundle to an 'un-bundled' package I put together.

(NB: this industry is constantly changing so these bundles will already be replaced by something else, but you'll get the idea. The value in telco is getting better and better so you have to shop around once in a while!)

EXAMPLE 1: Telstra + Foxtel bundle

For $159/month rising to $194/month after an initial discount, Telstra was offering:

- unlimited broadband data;
- 50Mbps speed;
- Foxtel Premium package with drama, sports and movies;
- a Telstra modem; and
- unlimited standard local, national and Australian mobile calls.

For a mobile plan, you could get the 180GB Telstra 'Essential' SIM-only plan for $68/month. (There was one cheaper plan but it had capped speeds.)

TOTAL COST: $227/month, rising to $262/month.

EXAMPLE 2: My home-made 'bundle'

For $65/month rising to $80/month, Tangerine was offering:

- unlimited broadband data;
- 50Mbps speed; and
- internet (VOIP) phone line (as you know by now, I think these are unnecessary but I've included it so we have a like-for-like comparison).

Instead of Foxtel, I subscribe to Kayo Sports and Binge, which have almost all the same sports and shows as the Premium package above because they're in fact owned by Foxtel, but they're priced from just $40/month.

For a mobile plan, I pay $30 for 55GB of data with amaysim, which includes local and international calls and unlimited data banking.

The only thing missing from my bundle is a modem, but Tangerine offers discounted Google Nest wi-fi modems starting from $180.

TOTAL COST: $135/month rising to $150/month.

THE VERDICT

The Telstra-Foxtel bundle costs an extra $92/month, or $1104/year to begin with. Then, as introductory discounts expire, the difference rises to $112/month, or $1344/year.

And that was based on 'new customer prices' in late 2022 – bear in mind that many old Telstra customers are still paying old Sleeping Beauty prices.

Insider Trick: The Squeaky Wheel

Aussies have a *lot* of complaints about our telcos. We had 167,831 in the 2017–2018 financial year (that's about one formal complaint to the ombudsman every three minutes), which then dropped to 127,000 complaints in the year before the pandemic, and skyrocketed by 1500% when COVID hit!

These are big businesses and your complaint is like one of those little penguins busting a gut to survive in the David Attenborough docos – you need to give it a leg-up.

I've found that the best way to get your telco's attention when there's a problem is to apply the sliding scale approach. First, ask to speak to a manager. If you get no result, then make it public (but polite) on their social media page. Still no joy? Make it official.

The TIO is your mate too. It stands for Telecommunications Industry Ombudsman. TIO opens a file when you make an official complaint, they give it a number, and they require your telco to open their own file and to put someone in charge of resolving it too. Bingo.

Your efforts to get some poor sod in a foreign call centre to fix your problem were valiant, but it was always a longshot. Now you've made your little penguin stand out from the colony.

Here's where to contact your new best mate TIO: www.tio.com.au/making-a-complaint

CHAPTER 16
STREAMING & PAY TV

> 'We compete with sleep. And we're winning.'
> **Netflix CEO Reed Hastings, when asked about the streaming service's biggest competitor.**

This is a new bill that we didn't need to worry about a decade ago.

Sure, about 40% of Aussie households had pay TV in the form of Foxtel, Austar or the older OptusVision (remember that?). But it was still a luxury, paid for by a minority.

Most of us bought albums and songs on CD or on iTunes and had a membership at the local Video Ezy or Blockbuster (remember them?).

Now, over 70% of Australian homes are streaming TV and movies and music and we're forking out over $2.7 billion a year on it.

As of 2022, the average home has 3.3 TV/movie subscriptions and 2 music subscriptions, which adds up to a bill of about $500–$600/year.

NUMBER CRUNCH

Aussies subscribed to 23.4 million streaming services in 2022. We had 6.3 million Netflix accounts, 4.1 million Amazon Prime Video accounts, 3 million Disney+ accounts, 2.5 million Stan accounts, 1.3 million Kayo Sports accounts, 1.3 million Binge accounts, 1.1 million Paramount+ accounts and 1 million Optus Sport accounts.

Source: Telsyte

So here's the problem: in the early days of Netflix, streaming WAS a money-saving hack in itself – dump pay TV, subscribe to a couple of streamers, save around $500 a year, laugh all the way to the bank.

That's still an easy saving for Foxtel subscribers. But now we all need to watch our streaming costs too. We've reached the era of 'peak streaming', where there's so much good content spread across more than 20 different platforms that, if you want to watch all of it, it'll cost you about $150/month – the same as a premium Foxtel subscription.

Prices are also rising – Netflix used to be $10/month for a standard subscription and now it's $14. So if we're not careful, our streaming bills can blow out and suck hundreds of dollars from our bank accounts like little vampires – even when we're not using them.

So let's look at how to keep these thirsty little suckers at bay.

In a nutshell

Potential saving	Up to $1000 for an average household
Easiest	'Ditching pay TV' and 'Freebies'
Next-easiest	'The off button' and 'Pick a winner'
Top tools	Google Chromecast
If I could tell you one thing about TV bills it would be:	You can stream almost everything on Foxtel for half the price elsewhere

DITCHING PAY TV

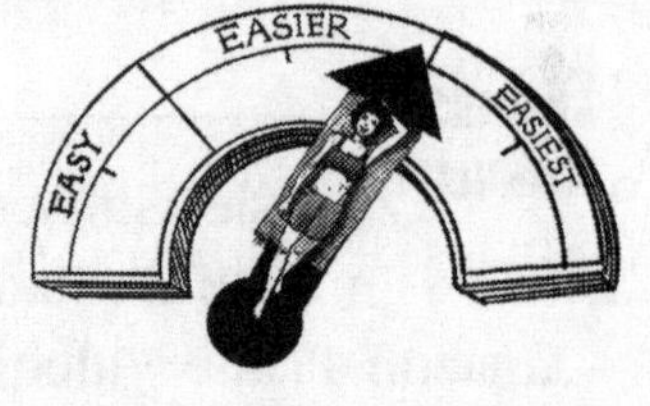

Potential saving: Up to $1000

First things first. If you're still paying for old school pay TV, why?

Even Foxtel has launched a few streaming services that carry most of the TV shows, sports and movies you get via the Foxtel cable or dish.

Kayo Sports has almost every sport on Foxtel. Binge has almost every TV show and movie on Foxtel.

Subscribe to both of them and the cost starts from $35/month, while a Foxtel package with both sport and drama will cost you $74/month outside of occasional honeymoon offers. That's over $400 a year of easy money back in your pocket.

If you took their news service too, called Flash, for $8/month, you'd get almost everything in a premium Foxtel package starting from $43 versus $140/month – over $1000 difference a year.

As I write this, Foxtel is offering all the content on its $140/month satellite package for a discounted $49/month via its Foxtel Now streaming service for the first year. It then rises to $104/month.

CHEAPEST OPTIONS COMPARED

	FOXTEL	STREAMING
Drama	$69/mth	$10/mth
Sport	$74/mth	$25/mth
Drama & Sport	$74/mth	$35/mth
Drama, Sport & News	$140/mth	$43/mth

There may be content on Foxtel that you cannot get on streaming – I've found some niche horse racing stuff, for example. The Foxtel IQ box technology is also excellent and it's been a reason for many to stay connected. But for most of us, Foxtel cable or satellite is an expensive white elephant – and even Foxtel knows it!

Too EASY!

How You Can Get All The Content You Want Without A Cable Or Even A Tv Aerial

The dilemma for a lot of Foxtel subscribers is how to get free-to-air TV if they cut the Foxtel cord, because many get ABC, SBS, 7, 9 and 10 through the pay TV cable or satellite dish.

I lived in two homes without a TV aerial within a year, so I had to find a solution to this one myself – and in the end it cost just $99.

If you buy the latest smart TV, it will have all the free-to-air TV apps installed and you can stream all of it live over the internet. But Google and Apple's smart TV devices – called Chromecast with Google TV and Apple TV 4K – will effectively transform your existing telly into the latest smart TV and toss in a few Google/Apple bonus features, too.

Both devices just plug into the back of your TV and offer access to all the major streaming services.

I chose Google because it's cheaper, and it allows you to 'cast' from both Apple and Android devices (Apple's Airplay only worked with Apple devices at the time of writing).

So, there you have it. For under $100 I now have access to all the free-to-air TV stations via their streaming apps. Plus, as an added bonus, the Google device communicates with my Google Nest wi-fi modem, which is voice activated, so I can even turn on the TV without hunting for the remote! Welcome to the future.

FREEBIES

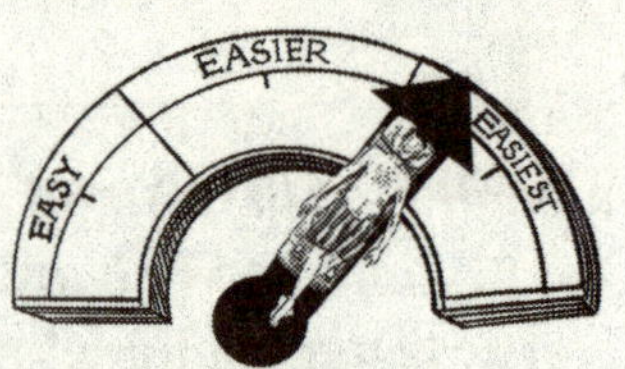

Potential saving: Up to $200
Of course, before you adopt all these other money-saving hacks, you should make sure you're taking all the freebies on offer.

Use ALL the free trials: Netflix canned its free trial a while back but the rest still offer them. If you took them all back to back you could watch FREE content for about five months and listen to FREE music for more than nine months before you had to pay a cent! Here are the major examples:

Amazon Prime Video – 30 days FREE
Stan – 30 days FREE
Stan Sport – 7 days FREE
Paramount+ – 7 days FREE
Apple TV+ – 7 days FREE
Hayu – 7 days FREE
Kayo Sports – 14 days FREE
Binge – 14 days FREE
Flash – 14 days FREE
Foxtel Now – 10 days FREE
Britbox – 7 days FREE

Music streamers oscillate back and forth between offering 1 month free or 3 months free but the best deals are:

Spotify (music) – 3 months FREE
Apple Music – 3 months FREE
Amazon Music Unlimited – 3 months FREE
Qobuz – 3 months FREE
Tidal – 3 months FREE

Get it free when you sign up to something else: Streaming services are becoming a popular add-on to other offers. Optus sometimes offers 12 months of Apple Music for free, Telstra might have 3 months of free Binge, Foxtel plans sometimes include free Netflix, and so on.

By the time you read this, those offers will probably have changed, but there'll be new ones about, so keep your eyes peeled.

Make the most of 100% FREE services: There are thousands of fantastic TV shows and movies available on 100% free streaming services, most of them owned by the free-to-air TV networks.

The ABC's iview has been one of the best streaming apps around for years now, and SBS's app, while a bit clunky at times, has more content on it than some of the paid services.

You need to create an account for most of these now, but there's no cost.

ABC iview – FREE and ad-free
SBS on Demand – FREE with ads
7Plus – FREE with ads
9Now – FREE with ads
10Play – FREE with ads
TUBI – FREE with ads

Insider Trick: The Elizabeth Taylor

Streaming is a new industry, but it's an ancient business model. In streaming land, here is what's written on the CEO's whiteboard:

1. Get them in on a great honeymoon deal such as a 'free trial' and capture their payment details.
2. Start charging them full price after the free trial ends.
3. Take a punt that most won't cancel, even if they're not using the service much.

But the honeymoon model creates a loophole for those who are cunning enough to leap through it.

You can do an Elizabeth Taylor and take honeymoon after honeymoon, or free trial after free trial, and watch months of free content – as long as you remember to cancel before the freebie ends.

If you do get plenty of use from the free trial and you decide to stay, well that's OK because this would qualify as an 'Angel subscription' that could save you spending more money elsewhere.

It's sometimes even possible to take more than one honeymoon with a single streaming service (let's call this the 'Richard Burton'). Let's just say you've got two or three email addresses, as many of us do, and multiple devices or device.

That means you can potentially enjoy two or three free trial periods with a streaming service, because they mostly identify you by your email address or device.

At the peak of the popularity of *Game of Thrones*, thousands of Aussies (including Yours Truly) used this trick to watch Season 8 in 2019 – signing up for a free 'honeymoon' trial on Foxtel Now after the first few episodes, bingeing them so we were up to speed, and then watching the final episodes in real time during the honeymoon trial period – before cancelling the $25 a month subscription soon afterwards.

No doubt many didn't cancel though, and maybe Foxtel Now ended up in front at the end of the day. Only they will know the answer to that one . . .

Share the love: It goes without saying that two people living in the same house should not be paying for two subscriptions to the same service. Whether you're a family or a share house or a hippy commune, it pays to get a subscription that allows more than one user simultaneously to share it. For example, two single-screen Netflix subscriptions cost $20 a month. One multi-screen subscription costs $14 a month and offers better picture quality. No-brainer! Spotify and Apple Music also have 'family' subscription options which you can share among up to six people.

Of course, millions of people are abusing this. It's a known fact that many of us share subscriptions with people we *don't* live with, and the streaming services don't like this – it's contrary to their terms of use. Netflix keeps threatening to crack down on it estimating that 100 million of its 220 million users are sharing subscriptions. But in most cases, it is technically possible. In some cases, the service will ask your address when you're added to a family subscription to confirm where you live, but in general it's very hard for them to know whether you all live in the same place.

True Story: Mike Teavee (Not His Real Name) Saves Almost $1000 By Sharing Subs

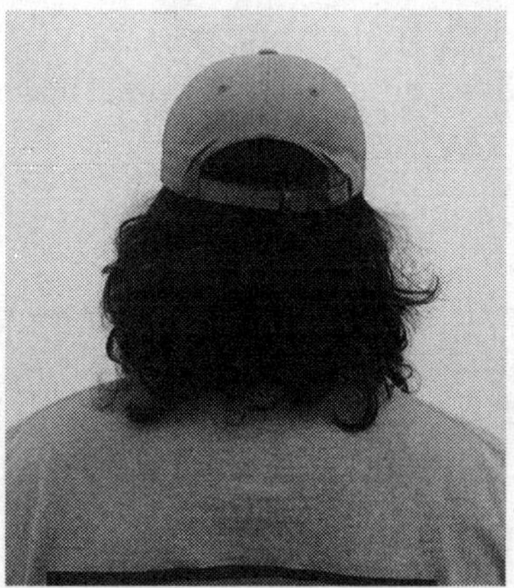

I once interviewed Mike Teavee (not his real name), who was saving almost $1000 a year by sharing subscriptions. Here's what he told me:

'My Dad, who lives in Asia, pays $US16 a month for a two-screen Netflix subscription, which five different people in three different countries use: there's Dad in Asia, me in Sydney, my two teenage cousins in WA, and my sister in Africa. Due to the time difference, we have virtually never been pinged for watching too many screens at once. It's great.

'My girlfriend pays $14 a month for Stan. Again, we have multiple people using the account. My girlfriend and I, our friend in Perth, my girlfriend's sister, brother, parents, and friend in Perth, and then my Dad in Asia – who uses it in return for lending us his Netflix login.

'I front the $25 a month for Kayo Sports. I use it every single day for live and on-demand sports and highlights. But I also give it to my friend in Perth and my dad in Asia (who can watch with a VPN).

'My friend in Perth (who's getting free Stan and Kayo Sports) comes in handy for access to Spotify. Wesley pays $18 a month for a Spotify family account. Me, my girlfriend, and two other friends of Wesley's all went into the Spotify settings on the computer and made our address the same as Wesley's. So we now all pay Wesley $3 a month for Spotify.'

All up, this sharing was saving Mike $444/year. But he's also a US sports nut and he shares subscriptions to the NHL, MLB and NFL too, which saves him an additional $535.

TOTAL ANNUAL SAVING: $979

Is it illegal? Not strictly speaking, but it is contrary to the terms of service, so they can kick you out if they catch you. I'm certainly not condoning it, but sharing is commonplace and this is the most extreme example I've come across.

PRO TIP

Buy in bulk and save 30%

Some services will give you almost 30% off for paying annually. If you know you'll use them all year, this can also be a way of locking in the price and avoiding any increases over the year (just remember to make a diary note to review them before they auto-renew):

Disney+ – $120/yr
Amazon Prime – $59/yr
Britbox – $90/yr

FIND THE 'OFF' BUTTON

Potential saving: Up to $300 for an average home

Maybe the most useful piece of info I can give you about streaming services is this: you can turn them on and off, like a TV!

Welcome to the world of 'stream-hoppers' – money-savvy TV aficionados who jump from one service to another, bingeing their favourite show and then moving on to the next, while pausing them in between.

It's entirely possible but they don't make it easy. It won't come as a surprise to learn that the 'off' switch for most streaming services is well-hidden, so here's a short guide to the major ones. (Note: I find it's always easier to do so by logging in on a computer rather than on your phone.)

Netflix: Log in on a computer > Click on the Netflix logo top left > Click on the dropdown arrow top right > Select 'Account' > Click on the grey 'Cancel membership' button on the left.

Amazon Prime: Log in on a computer > Click on the icon top right > Select 'Account & Settings' > Click 'Edit on Amazon' > Click 'Account & Lists' top right > Click 'Your Prime Membership' > Click 'Update, cancel & more'.

Spotify: Log in on a computer > Click on the 'Profile' dropdown menu top right > Select 'Account' > Scroll down and click 'Subscription' on the left-hand side > Click 'Change or cancel'.

Apple Music: Log in on a computer > Open iTunes > Click on 'Account' in the menu at the top of the screen > Select 'View my account' > Scroll down to settings, find the word 'Subscriptions' and click 'Manage' > Click the button that says 'Cancel'.

You can return any time. Most services will remember your likes and dislikes and other data for more than six months. Some will even offer you another free trial to come back.

PRO TIP

When you cancel, you're not cut off immediately – if you've paid for a month, you'll be cut off at the end of a month. So you can subscribe and cancel immediately if you're worried about remembering to do so later.

Sometimes they'll even 'pay' you to come back!

I've dabbled with both Spotify and Apple Music in the past. In the end we settled on a Spotify family subscription but I think both have their strengths.

While researching this I went back for a closer look at Apple Music and noticed they were offering me 'one month free' to come back, even though I'd cancelled in the past.

So I took it for the month and decided I'd try them both out again for a while and see which one I preferred.

And yes – I did remember to cancel one of them after the free month. I've also heard of Netflix offering people a second free trial if they didn't complete their first one.

Insider Trick: The De Niro

I once met a wise old codger at a One Big Switch member event who told me why he didn't like to pay anything by direct debit. 'It's like they've got their hand in me pocket!' he explained, and he was dead right.

Direct debit is convenient and you'll often get a better deal by agreeing to use it, but it does have inherent dangers.

If the provider gets something wrong, for example, they can charge you before you've had a chance to review the bill. And then the onus is on you to claw the money back. 'Possession is nine tenths of the law,' as the saying goes.

And it also puts the onus on you to keep checking if you're still getting value from the service and it hasn't become a 'Vampire subscription' – because as sure as night follows day, they're gonna keep charging you for it until you say stop!

PICK A WINNER

Potential saving: Up to $200

Here's a simple rule we came up with for our family of four to stop our streaming habit from spiraling out of control. I call it the 'Pick a Winner' rule.

Each member of the family is allowed to pick one streaming service at a time and only one. If we stick to it, we're signed up for four services at any given time and no more.

In one month, for example, my 10-year-old might pick Stan for All Blacks games, my 12-year-old might pick Binge for *Modern Family*, my wife and I might pick Apple TV+ for *Ted Lasso* and Kayo Sports for the footy.

With the footy season winding up, I might cancel Kayo Sports for now and sign up to Netflix for *Animal Kingdom*, and so on.

NUMBER CRUNCH

Reviews.org has estimated the cost of streaming over a lifetime at $19,300 and found that just cancelling one service could save you almost $10,000 over time.

Here's another way to decide which subscriptions to keep and which ones to switch off:

- Draw a line down the middle of a page to create two columns. Call one of them 'Angel Subs' and call the other one 'Vampire Subs'. Put each of your subscriptions in one column or the other.

- Angels are the subscriptions that save you money, compared to what you'd pay otherwise for renting TV, movies, music, etcetera on an ad hoc basis.
- Vampire subscriptions – just like they sound – are the ones that cost you money by sucking it out of your direct debit account without giving you real value in return.
- Then, drive a stake through the heart of all the Vampire Subs (or at least the ones you can live without) and cancel them. Don't worry – you can always come back.

CONSUMER PSYCHOLOGY 101: Why financial types love subscription businesses

It's not limited to TV, movies and music . . . Subscription businesses are now exploding into a broad range of industries that never had them before – from clothes to pet food and even toilet paper – thanks to a combination of easier payment technologies, slicker delivery, and the push to live more sustainably and use less.

Here are some examples of the things you can now get via subscription:

Product	**Examples**
TV and movies	Netflix, Disney+, Stan, Binge, Amazon Prime
Music	Spotify, Apple Music
News	*Sydney Morning Herald*, *The Age*, *Herald Sun*, *Daily Telegraph*
Gyms	Fitness First, F45
Theatre/Opera/Ballet	Check your local theatres
Audiobooks	Audible.com
Cars	GoGet.com.au and CarBar.com.au
Clothes	GlamCorner.com.au

SodaStream gas	Bubble
Surfboards and skis	AwayCo.com
Razors	Au.DollarShaveClub.com
Toilet paper	Au.WhoGivesACrap.org
Pet food	PetCircle.com.au

Financial types love subscription businesses, because they meet the definition of a 'good business': they make money while you sleep. (Not you, the customer, of course, but you, the business owner ...)

They're built on the back of a human trait that psychologists and economists call 'status quo bias', which describes our innate human aversion to change.

Subscription businesses know that if they can just get us on the hook – often with a honeymoon deal such as 'one month free' or 'half price for six months' – human nature dictates that many of us won't cancel, even if we stop using the service. But if we can understand this 'subscription trap' and get our heads around a few simple tricks to avoid it, we can kill not just this bill but any others that are based on a subscription model, from newspapers and news websites, to superannuation and online photo storage.

A FEW MORE WAYS TO SAVE A BUCK ON STREAMING:

Do you need HD?

You can save yourself almost $50 a year (and give your data plan a break) by downgrading to a basic plan if you only watch one screen at a time and don't need HD (high-definition) picture quality.

Pick a mobile provider that offers 'unmetered' streaming for your chosen service

This means that all or some downloads from Netflix or iview or Apple Music or whichever service it applies to do *not* count towards your download limit. So you could potentially take out a cheaper plan than you would otherwise and still watch TV on your bus ride home.

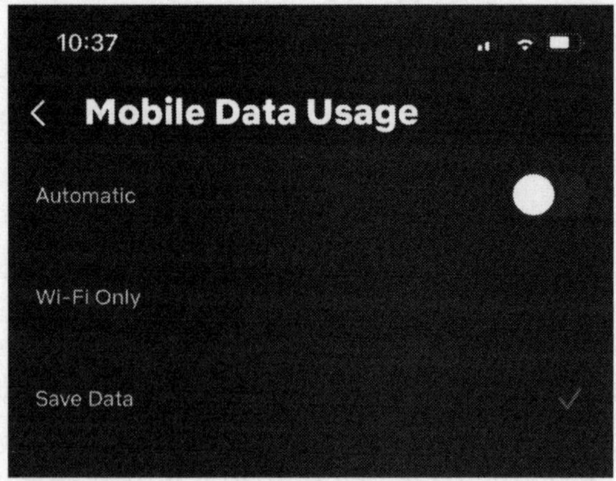

Change your mobile settings to use less data

Most apps allow you to set how data-intensive you want the stream to be. For example, the automatic setting on Netflix gives you about four hours per GB of data. However, if you click the icon at the top right in the app and then go to 'App Settings' > 'Mobile Data Usage', you can switch to 'Save Data' which gives you about six hours per GB of data. Or 'Wi-Fi Only' which means it'll only work when connected to a wi-fi network.

DOWO: Download online, watch offline

When we go on long car trips, we make sure we download a movie for the kids to watch before we leave home and then they watch it offline in the car when they get sick of playing 'I Spy'. Note that this only works for certain shows on certain devices, so your best bet is to go to the help section of the app and search for 'Download and watch offline'.

Don't subscribe to multiple music streaming services

The TV services mostly have exclusivity over certain content, but the music ones mostly don't. In other words, the music selection you get from the different services is largely the same. So the main thing to look at when it comes to music streaming is whether you like the design of the platform and what your family and friends use – because you might want to share a subscription or playlist with them.

CHAPTER 17
CAR & HOME INSURANCE

'Face it girls, I'm older and I have more insurance.'
Kathy Bates as Evelyn Couch in *Fried Green Tomatoes*,
after she crashes into two girls who beat her to a parking spot and say, *'Face it lady, we're younger and faster'*.

When I was growing up, I had a friend who was a bit wild. He used to jump off his second-floor balcony into his pool and he was crazy-brave on a skateboard or a surfboard – basically, he was every mother-of-a-teenage-boy's worst nightmare.

So imagine my surprise when he finished school and became an insurance broker! Talk about poacher turned gamekeeper . . .

You see, I have a theory that we all have a degree of risk that we're comfortable with in life, and that determines our attitude to insurance too.

Some of us can't get out of bed in the morning without comprehensive insurance cover, while others can live with the bare minimum – or none at all.

And each to their own. I'm not here to tell you what the right level of cover is for you, but I am here to make sure you don't overpay for it. Because there's a lot of fat in some insurance premiums, particularly if you're a Sleeping Beauty with one of the big established brands and you've just been dutifully paying the slightly higher premium they send you each year without ever asking any questions (which is 2 in 3 of us, incidentally – but it used to be 4 in 5 so we're getting better).

Roy Morgan research says the brands with the most loyal customers are RACV, Apia, CGU, RACQ, Suncorp, CBA and NRMA – in that order.

Some of those brands were the same ones that raised home insurance premiums by an average 15% in 2022 – the biggest hikes in 9 years, thanks to the February floods.

Car and home insurers have fought tooth and nail to make it hard for us to compare prices easily online in the way we can energy or telco plans. This industry is stuck in the dark ages when it comes to transparency.

But sometimes, almost-identical policies can differ by over $1000 a year – so let's run through the simplest ways to make sure you're not getting fleeced. As always, we'll start with the easiest.

In a nutshell

Potential saving	Anywhere from $100 up to $1000 for an average household
Easiest	'Mystery-Shopping' and 'Switching'
Next-easiest	'Tweak your policy'
Top tools	Your own insurer's website and cheap challenger brands such as BudgetDirect.com.au, Youi.com.au or WoolworthsInsurance.com.au
If I could tell you one thing about insurance bills it would be:	Pay the 'new customer' price, not the 'Sleeping Beauty' price

MYSTERY-SHOPPING

Potential saving: Up to $400, depending on your home and car

The 'Mystery-Shopper' is the #1 insider trick you'll need to win the war on this particular household bill.

The Mystery-Shopper involves you donning the disguise of a new customer and seeing whether you get better treatment. If you get better treatment when you look new and shiny, you can use that to demand they treat little 'old' you just the same.

1. **Grab your renewal.** Thanks to some recent changes to the law it should show you both this year's premium and last year's and the percentage increase. If not, use this formula:

$$\frac{\text{(This year's premium minus last year's premium)} \times 100}{\text{Last year's premium}}$$

2. **Go to your own insurer's website.** Pretend you're a new customer and get a quote using *most* of the same details as your current policy (you might have to 'disguise' yourself with your neighbour's address or by not entering your licence plate as they will probably have yours saved).

Compare the two. Are they charging you more than a new customer? If so, why should you be punished for your loyalty?

At this point, you can call your provider, present them with the evidence and ask them to match the price you've been quoted online. The simplest way to save, after all, is just to get a better deal from your current provider.

But if you want to maximise your saving, I'd recommend taking the next step too and getting a quote from one of their competitors.

NUMBER CRUNCH

Allan Fels is a former head of the ACCC. More recently, as 'The NSW Emergency Services Levy Insurance Monitor', he compared what the top ten home insurers charged their new customers versus their 'loyal' renewing customers and found that, on average, *renewing customers paid a 'loyalty tax'* of 34% more.

He also found that 'quotes range from say $1000 to $2700 for the same house and contents at a specified address'.

'It seems that like banks and energy companies, insurers count on the loyalty of existing customers to offer discounts to new ones,' Professor Fels said.

'This really translates to a simple message for consumers – don't assume you are getting the best deal with your renewals. Always check the prices of other suppliers, and if your insurer is out of line, go elsewhere.'

Source: *The Sydney Morning Herald*

Insider Trick: The Red Dog

This insider trick is about those rare cases where loyalty *does* in fact pay. To be fair, car and home insurers were one of the first industries to offer rewards for loyal customers.

Multi-policy discounts and no-claim bonuses were early examples of reward and loyalty schemes. These are still offered by some providers, but not all – and they can be valuable.

But DO check: don't simply assume you're paying less because you're on one of these policies. Even if you're receiving these bonuses, you might still be paying more.

As the case study on the next page shows, even a 25% multi-policy discount is sometimes more expensive than 'new customer' prices from a challenger brand – but not always.

Case Study: Loyalty discounts versus cheap challenger brands

NRMA has long been one of the insurers that pioneered multi-policy loyalty discounts.

These days they'll give you up to 25% off some policies if you've been with them for 25+ years or more and you have 10+ policies. (Although who has this many insurance policies, I'm not quite sure. John Laws, maybe?)

To see whether that discount would make the cover as cheap as a challenger brand that is very price-focused, such as Budget Direct, I did a comparison in 2018 when writing *KILL BILLS!*.

Four years later, I did the same comparison and the result was very different.

I got quotes from both websites for comprehensive insurance using the same details for my own Hyundai – aged first 6 and then 10 years old. I included roadside assistance each time and either the full 25% loyalty discount from NRMA or the 15% new customer discount from Budget – and the results were as follows . . .

	2018	**2022**
NRMA	$911	$768
Budget Direct	$743	$927

What can we take away from this little experiment? One, multi-policy discounts are pretty useless if the original price is too high, so you do have to do a sense-check. Two, sometimes they do add up – it all depends on your address, your car and your driving record. And three, insurers change their pricing regularly to target different 'customer segments' so it pays to look around.

(NB: These are just quotes for my particular details and they don't represent all of NRMA's pricing or Budget Direct's pricing. Your results could be different.)

SWITCHING

Potential saving: Up to $1000, depending on your home and car

Get another quote. You could try an insurer that's been recommended by a friend or that you have another policy with. You could go to one of the 'challenger brand' websites, such as Budget Direct, Youi or Woolworths Insurance. They're generally pretty cheap. Or you could ask a comparison website such as Compare the Market or Canstar to get a quote for you. If you can't decide, maybe check out the latest awards or star ratings for value at a website such as Canstar.com.au or Money Magazine and see who they've rated highly in the past year.

PRO TIP

Once you get these online quotes, sometimes it pays to wait 24 hours! Some insurers will do what's called an 'abandon cart' offer of, say, a $50 gift card if you don't accept their quote straight away. So if you've got a day up your sleeve, just wait and see if their offer suddenly improves overnight.

The reason I suggest you take this extra step is that you'll have a bit of extra leverage when you call your provider – and you'll have a fallback option if they refuse to play ball.

Remember: you're not locked in! You can switch car or home insurance anytime, even if you've paid for the year. You're generally entitled to a refund of unused premium – just as you'd get if you sold the car or home and moved, for example. So don't pass up a good deal just because your renewal isn't due yet.

Here's the script for when you ring up your insurance company:

'Hi, my name's [Groucho Marx/Robert De Niro/Insert real name here] and I've been a loyal customer of yours for ______ years. I've recently received my renewal notice. I couldn't help noticing that it's gone up by _____. And I also couldn't help noticing that it's ______ more than you're charging a new customer with similar details to me. I know this because I got a quote on your website for a new policy with my details and I must have accidentally put my neighbour's address in. Oops! Anyway, the quote came in at _____. How is that fair? I'd like you to match that new customer price please, and if you can I'll renew right now. If you can't, I've got a quote from another provider and I'm tempted to take my business elsewhere.'

INSIDE INFO

The home and car insurance markets in Australia are dominated by four main insurers who make up approximately three-quarters of policies and in some cases, they own multiple brands.

IAG Group owns NRMA, RACV, Coles Insurance, SGIO, SGIC, WFI, CGU and others. Suncorp Group owns Suncorp, AAMI, GIO, Bingle, APIA, Shannons, Terry Scheer and others. QBE and Allianz round out the 'Big Four'.

There are comparison websites comparing brands outside the Big Four but the insurance giants do not let them compare the brands above because they are opposed to comparison websites, even though they exist in the UK, Norway, Ireland, the US and that most remote of foreign countries: northern Australia (where the government intervened to build one because it became so hard to get affordable insurance after the cyclones and floods of the last decade).

The industry says that comparing insurance policies based on price will lead us to downgrade our cover without realising it and we could end up under-insured – and they might have a point.

But it would also expose the insurance industry's dirty little secret, which is the enormous gap in prices between some insurers, and between new and old customers.

Some of the established big brands would lose a lot of customers if it was easy to see how much more they are charging their Sleeping Beauties.

The big guys defend themselves by saying that their cover is superior, and sometimes that's true too. But most insurance policies are about 90% identical to each other – it's really only a handful of details that differentiate them.

And once you look closely at those for yourself, you might decide those differences are not worth paying extra for.

Insider Trick: The Elizabeth Taylor

Insurance is another one of those industries that operates mostly on the 'Honeymoon Strategy' business model: they win new customers over with a very cheap one-year premium and then hope to make money out of you in later years if you don't leave.

Most of us stay, because we can't be bothered, and it works for the insurance companies.

But like power companies and telcos, it's possible to do an 'Elizabeth Taylor' when dealing with insurers and move regularly, thereby enjoying honeymoon after honeymoon.

Liz married Richard Burton twice, and you might find you leave and later return to the same insurance company – which is fine. Who am I to judge? Or you might threaten to leave and then get retained by a better offer, which is also a win.

Don't worry. It's not like a real marriage. Just go looking for Mr or Miss Right-for-Now, and if you get a better offer, dump them.

The only possible downside is that some insurers have schemes that reward loyalty, so do make sure you weigh that up against what's on offer elsewhere.

True Stories: Why You Should Never Take The First Offer

Ashley, a doctor from the Southern Highlands in NSW, bought a new car and took out an insurance policy through the car dealership. It cost him $1450 for the first year.

When he got his renewal, he shopped around and halved his premium to $686. He'd had no idea he was over-paying.

Sylvia's home insurance premium shot up by around 50% during the price hikes of 2022, so she contacted a comparison website and they got her a quote that was around half of her renewal, WITH THE SAME INSURER! She couldn't believe it.

I've had a similar experience – although not as extreme as those. When my home insurer sent me a 6% increase, I did a mystery-shop and got a 'new customer' quote on their website that was 22% cheaper.

So I told the call centre consultant and they said they couldn't drop my price by that much, but could I hold on a second while they speak to their supervisor . . .?

A few minutes later they came back on the line and said they could cancel my current policy and create me a new one with the new customer pricing. So I said, 'Go for it!'

The moral of these stories? Never take the first offer; new customers often get better prices; loyalty isn't rewarded; and it pays to whinge politely.

TWEAK YOUR POLICY

Potential saving: Up to $300, depending on your home and car

There are a few things you can do to get your premium down – not all of them will work for you but here are some ideas to consider.

Pay annually, if you can: Paying by the month is popular, but some insurers will charge you as much as 30% extra over the course of a year for the privilege. It may be difficult to pay for a year all at once, but if you can do so, you could save big time.

Raise your excess: Your 'excess' is the amount you have to pay if you decide to make a claim on your policy. The Insurance Council of Australia explains: 'If your home is damaged in a storm, the cost of repairing the damage might be $4000. If you had a $600 excess, you'd pay the first $600 and the insurer would pay the remainder.' Most insurance policies have a standard excess that you can increase if you want, which will bring down the regular premium you pay. Excesses can range from about $500 up to $2000. Basically, you're making a bet that you won't have to claim.

PRO TIP

For a 5-year-old Toyota Corolla, increasing your excess by $500 can cut your premium by about $100 a year.

Jewellery and other valuables: For contents insurance, you usually have to nominate items valued at over $1000 or a similar amount. If you have a lot of family heirlooms, they could be pushing up your premium substantially. Why not look into the cost of a safe deposit box for valuables you almost never wear, to increase their security and cut the cost of your contents cover?

Don't insure twice: If you take out 'portable contents cover' as part of your home insurance, your devices and other valuables could be covered even if they're stolen or damaged when you take them out. But keep in mind that you might have some cover for them under your car insurance too – so don't 'over-insure' them if it's unnecessary.

Younger drivers: Insuring younger drivers can push up the cost of insurance substantially. If you have to add an under-25 driver to a policy, there are a few ways to minimise the cost. Choose a small car with a small engine, if possible (Young Driver + Big Engine = Big Premium). Choose a locally made car where you can (Young Driver + European Parts = Big Premium). And if possible, add them to a policy on a new or newish car. Insurance premiums, as a percentage of the value of the car, are significantly lower for new cars – this is based on the common view that young drivers in new cars are a better risk. If you really want to get your premium down, remove younger drivers altogether from the cover. Some insurers allow you to say no one under 25 or 35 or even 50 is going to drive the car, and they'll then drop the price of insurance. This won't go down well if you've got teenage kids! But if they're all grown up, go for it.

Join a group-buying club or savings club: Membership of a group like One Big Switch or motoring organisations such as the NRMA, RACQ, RACV, RAA or RAC WA can unlock group-discounted offers on home and contents insurance or car insurance that you can use as a jumping-off point for your research.

Loyalty discounts: If you've stuck with the same provider for years, then why not call them up and ask for a loyalty discount, even if they don't advertise them? Stranger things have been known to happen.

Security: By installing better security (even just locks on your windows or an alarm on your house or car) you can also reduce your insurance premium. Insurers take all these things into account when working out your price.

Conduct a risk assessment: De-risk your car or home and it could save you on your premium. Clutter, dodgy wiring, overgrown gardens, leaves in the guttering right through to pools and dangerous appliances are all potential hazards, which can lead to a claim and a higher premium. In some cases, hazards such as a tree near your house will increase your premium, so it might pay to trim it back.

Estimate realistically: Don't overvalue your personal items and belongings just because of their emotional connection to you. The bigger the price tag you put on them, the more you pay in coverage. Many insurers have a 'house and contents value estimator' on their website, but I'm a bit suss about these tools. Your contents always seem to come out at a higher value than you expected. Which means you pay the insurance company more to cover them. And who created the estimator tool? The insurance company! Funny about that.

Drive less, pay less: Certain insurers now have policies designed for customers who drive very little. If you tell these insurers your average car usage, they may be able to lower your premium.

Prove you're a good driver: If you complete a certified 'advanced driving course', some insurers will lower your premium (especially if you're young). These courses last about four to five hours and are a good idea: you'll learn how to brake suddenly, how to handle high speed and dangerous conditions, and you might even have a bit of fun. Also, some insurers now use GPS devices to see how good a driver you are: if you don't mind 'Big Brother' checking up on you, they monitor data on your speed, distance travelled and braking.

FAQs

How much should I insure my house for?

This is a tough one. Most of us aren't builders. We don't automatically know what it'd cost to rebuild our home or replace our car. But don't just take a stab in the dark. After the 'Black Saturday' Victorian bushfires in the summer of 2009, an estimated 13% of homes which required reconstruction or significant repair weren't adequately insured, according to ASIC Moneysmart. And many of those who lost their homes in the Sydney bushfires of 2013 were also unable to rebuild them because they didn't have sufficient coverage.

The insurance industry recommends a calculator created by real estate data company Core Logic, which I think looks pretty reliable: UnderstandInsurance.com.au/calculator/building-calculator

If you live in a danger zone and want total peace of mind, consider taking out what's known as a 'Total Replacement Policy', where the insurer agrees to repair or rebuild your home to its current standard. It might be a little dearer. Your call.

How much should I insure my car for?

This is also a tough question but there's lots of help available online. A website such as Redbook (Redbook.com.au) will tell you the average trade-in and private sale value of your car.

Most insurers will suggest a 'market value' when you get a quote, based on the car details you give them. *Check it!* Sometimes they get the price down by insuring your car for way less than its *real* market value.

You then need to decide whether to insure it for their 'market value' or an 'agreed value', which is an amount *you* suggest. If you're confident you know what the real value is, or what you're happy to receive if the car is written off, this can be a good option for you.

What about all these 'special features' they're offering me?

They're the insurance equivalent of the McDonald's upsell: 'Do you want fries with that?' Many providers offer these as additions to the standard cover, and if you want to keep your costs down you could maybe do without them. They can include burnout of electric motors, accidental damage, public liability and windscreen cover. In the end, the rule is the same as it is with ALL insurance: you've got to decide what's useful to *you* based on your lifestyle and what's a waste of money.

The traditional view of insurance is that it's there to cover you for catastrophic losses that you can't afford to fix: a house burning down or being flooded, a major robbery maybe or a big car accident.

But insurers have found more and more small mishaps to cover over the years, even if you could probably afford to fix those yourself.

Here is a list of eight popular 'upsells' and what they cover:

1. Flood cover – this is defined as the covering of normally dry land by water that has escaped or been released from lakes, rivers, creeks or other natural watercourse. If you need flood cover, make sure you take up a policy that includes it, or buy it as an add-on.
2. Personal possessions – this covers those everyday valuable items such as mobile devices and jewellery that you sometimes carry around with you. They might already be covered by your policy in the car or home, but in some cases, these high-valued items can also be covered when you're away from the home as an add-on.
3. Accidental damage – a popular extra for those with young kids or grandkids! Most policies only cover damage from so-called 'insurance events', such as fire, explosion, theft or malicious damage (but not backyard cricket, for example). Most policies will not cover accidental loss or damage, except as an add-on.
4. Home emergency – entitles you to have an on-call tradesperson come to your rescue and fix that leaky shower pipe or blocked toilet.
5. Motor burnout cover – this is also known as 'fusion damage cover'. This covers you when the motor in household appliances such as your fridge, freezer or washing machine dies. A power surge or lightning strike can cause this, but do you think it's likely enough to pay extra for? It's up to you.

6. Windscreen cover – this reduces the cost of having a windscreen fixed if it gets chipped or cracked (which is common on open roads). Fixing a windscreen chip can cost about $200 and replacing a whole windscreen can cost over $1000 depending on the make of the car. So it's not a bad idea if you're driving long distances.
7. Roadside assistance – probably one of the more useful 'up-sell' items, unless you already have it from the manufacturer or dealer or a motoring club. Most new cars rarely break down but when they do, these guys are a godsend.
8. Hire car cover – covers the costs related to hiring a car while your car is under repair or out of action. Do you really need it? It depends on your circumstances. Sometimes it's included as standard anyway.

Do I have flood cover?

Again, you've gotta check! Don't assume anything where insurance is concerned. This is not standard on all policies and usually adds to the premium if you require it. Read the PDS, as they say in all the legalese!

What exactly does flood cover include?

Good question. People have been left high and dry in the past because of disagreements over the definition of what a flood is. Many of the Brisbane flood victims of 2011 found they were not fully covered, leading the federal government in 2012 to introduce a standard definition of 'flood' to help establish greater certainty for both insurers and policyholders. The newish industry-wide definition of flood is now: 'The covering of normally dry land by water that has escaped or been released from the normal confines of: any lake, or any river, creek or other natural watercourse, whether or not altered or modified; or any reservoir, canal or dam.' The Insurance Council of Australia says the difference between 'storm' and 'flood' damage is now clear: 'The storm might fill the river, but once the river overflows, that's a flood.'

CHAPTER 18
HEALTH INSURANCE

> 'If saving money is wrong, I don't want to be right!'
> **William Shatner**

The health insurance funds had a 'good pandemic,' as the saying goes. Before COVID-19 struck, this industry was in a real pickle. Premiums kept rising year after year and younger people were dropping out, meaning there was less money to fund the older customers who make most of the claims.

NUMBER CRUNCH

A $2000 policy in the days of Kevin Rudd PM would now cost over $4100, thanks to the cumulative impact of premium increases.

Commentators were warning of a 'death spiral' that could send health funds broke. But not anymore. In the two years after the pandemic arrived, 480,888 new people took out health insurance policies. The theory is that we're more concerned about our health since COVID-19, and elective surgery waiting lists have blown out to over 50,000 people in some states.

Health insurance is a big bill – it's behind only the mortgage/rent and groceries in many households, about equal to the average petrol bill and double the average power bill.

So, with over 11.5 million of us now paying through the nose for private health cover, some easy money-saving strategies have never been more vital.

As usual, let's start with the simplest ones.

In a nutshell

Potential saving	Anywhere from $50 up to $1000
Easiest	'Tweaking your policy' and 'Switching'
Next-easiest	Avoiding big gap payments
Top tools	The Gold-Silver-Bronze system and comparison websites
If I could tell you one thing about health insurance bills it would be:	You can switch and take as many 'new customer' offers as you like.

TWEAK YOUR POLICY

Potential saving: Up to $800

With premiums soaring since about 2005, millions of Australians have had to find ways to cut the cost of this bill. There are quite a few tweaks you can make – try these for starters:

Give your cover an annual check-up: Are you finished having children and still paying for obstetrics cover? Are you fit as a fiddle and paying for gastric banding cover? If you don't know the answer, you're not alone ... Many of us haven't reviewed our policy in years and could be paying hundreds extra for cover we don't need. Downgrading might be an option that could save you money. For example, removing obstetrics, IVF and pregnancy services from a policy saves about $500 p.a. for a family, on average. Some funds offer high-level covers without IVF or pregnancy, while some do not. Ask your fund if they do, or use the expertise of a comparison service.

Too EASY!

YOUR NEW WEAPON WHEN COMPARING HEALTH INSURANCE POLICIES

It used to be almost impossible to compare one health fund's policies to another, so in 2020 the federal government brought in a new system where every plan has to be labelled either Gold, Silver, Bronze or Basic.

Each category MUST include cover for certain treatments, so it's now far easier to decide which level of cover you need.

For example, if you need cover for joint replacements, pregnancy or sleep studies, you'll need a Gold policy.

Silver policies don't need to include those, but they do need to include cover for heart, lung and back procedures.

There's a full fact sheet available at PrivateHealth.gov.au but here's a high-level summary:

TREATMENTS	BRONZE	SILVER	GOLD
Rehab	✓	✓	✓
Psychiatric	✓	✓	✓
Palliative	✓	✓	✓
Brain, nervous system	✓	✓	✓
Eye (not cataracts)	✓	✓	✓
Ear, nose, throat	✓	✓	✓
Tonsils, adenoids	✓	✓	✓
Bone, joint, muscle	✓	✓	✓
Joint reconstructions	✓	✓	✓
Kidney, bladder	✓	✓	✓
Male reproductive	✓	✓	✓

Digestive system	✓	✓	✓
Hernia, appendix	✓	✓	✓
Gastro endoscopy	✓	✓	✓
Gynaecology	✓	✓	✓
Miscarriage, termination	✓	✓	✓
Cancer treatments	✓	✓	✓
Pain management	✓	✓	✓
Skin	✓	✓	✓
Breast	✓	✓	✓
Diabetes (not insulin pumps)	✓	✓	✓
Heart, vascular		✓	✓
Lung, chest		✓	✓
Blood		✓	✓
Back, neck, spine		✓	✓
Plastic, reconstructive		✓	✓
Dental surgery		✓	✓
Podiatric surgery		✓	✓
Hearing devices		✓	✓
Cataracts			✓
Joint replacements			✓
Dialysis			✓
Pregnancy, birth			✓
Assisted reproductive			✓
Weight loss surgery			✓
Insulin pumps			✓
Pain management devices			✓
Sleep studies			✓

Increase your excess: As with all insurance, if you're willing to agree to pay a higher 'excess' if you have to go to hospital, you can also get your premium down by hundreds of dollars.

For health insurance, 'an excess is an amount that you agree to pay towards the cost of hospital treatment, in exchange for lower premium costs'.

You may be required to pay an excess every time you go to hospital, or only the first time each year – it depends on the policy. But if you're not a regular visitor to hospital, a higher excess might be a good option for you to save some money.

In 2020, the maximum excess increased to $750 for a single or $1500 for a couple or family, so take advantage if it works for you.

Either use your extras, or dump them: If you have an 'Extras' policy, you need to use it. Claim as often as possible on things like dental, optometry, physio and so on – until you reach your annual limits. Get a massage that's classified as a 'remedial massage' from a therapist who's registered with your health fund. Go to a dentist who's covered entirely by your fund, or who at least has a deal with your fund to minimise your out-of-pocket costs. And make sure you get a pair of glasses or prescription sunnies every year. You can check how much you've claimed in the past year or two by asking your fund and if it's much less than the extras portion of your premium, consider dumping it!

PRO TIP

Having a 'Hospital' policy can help you avoid certain penalties and taxes, but 'Extras' policies are irrelevant at tax time. So only pay for them if you're getting your money's worth.

Pay annually, ideally the day BEFORE premium increases take effect: If you pay annually just before 1 April, when all health funds usually raise their premiums, you pay the *old* price for the coming year and you effectively postpone any price rise for 12 months. Good trick, if you can afford it.

Pay by direct debit: Some health funds such as NIB, GMHBA and Australian Unity also offer discounts of up to 4% for paying by direct debit, so consider doing this – and combining it with the trick above.

'Divorce' or 'marry' your policies: There are some quirks in the way policies are priced that you might be able to exploit as money-saving loopholes. For example, if you're in a couple and you have two singles policies, it might cost less to 'marry' your policies into one – as long as you both want roughly the same level of cover. On the other hand, if one of you wants Gold cover and the other only Basic or Bronze, see if it's cheaper to 'divorce' your policies. Ditto if one of you has a big 'lifetime health cover loading', which can add up to 70% to the cost of a policy – you might be better off having two singles policies so that the loading doesn't get applied to both of you. The other quirk is that couples policies usually cost the same as family policies, but family policies cover an unlimited number of children. So it's usually cheaper for people in their 20s, for example, to stay on the family plan for as long as possible, rather than take out their own policy.

Dump it altogether: It's always an option to simply rely on the public health system, which has its limitations but is still one of the best in the world if you live in the major cities. There could be some tax implications (more on those below) but if you are really struggling to afford private health cover, remember that at the end of the day, it's optional. Some households choose to self-insure instead and put some money aside in an emergency fund each month. Others rely on Medicare, which we've already paid for with our taxes.

SWITCHING

Potential saving: Up to $1000

EASY
EASIER
EASIEST

Switching can be a way to save money TWICE on your health insurance. First, you can sometimes find a similar policy for hundreds of dollars less, and second, when you switch you can sometimes get a bonus for new customers. These deals have kaboomed in recent years and now feature as much as $800 or even 12 weeks free for switchers.

INSIDE INFO

The law in Australia protects health insurance customers in a number of ways that can create money-saving loopholes. For example, it says that health insurance must be 'community-rated', which means that health funds cannot reject anyone who applies for cover and they cannot charge one person more than another person based on their health status. This means anyone can get just about any health insurance deal that is advertised. The law also says your policy must be 'portable', like a mobile phone number. If you switch to the same level of cover with another health fund, you take with you any waiting periods you've served plus any extras limits you haven't used yet in that year. This is also good for switchers because it means there's no cost for moving when you see a better deal.

Here's the drill.

1. **Once you've decided which level of cover you're after, it's time to shop around.** Health insurance is not one of the easiest bills to compare so don't be a hero! Ask for some help from a free comparison service if you need it. Go to Comparethemarket.com.au or CompareClub.com.au (which both cover a range of health funds but not all of them). They require a phone number and they'll ring you anyway, so you may as well just cut to the chase and call them yourself. Tell them what you need and see what policy they recommend.
2. **Now wait!** Don't accept their recommendation on the spot. Ask them to email it to you. Go to the provider's website and to OneBigSwitch.com.au to see if they have a special offer available

on that policy. These can include anything from '1 Month Free' to '12 Weeks Free', gift cards valued from $100 to $800, and even discounts of up to 12%. Sometimes they're only for members of certain groups such as motoring and consumer clubs.

3. Switch or stay? At this point, you can switch to the policy you've chosen or phone your current health fund and tell them you've got one foot out the door. Some funds will give you a discount on the spot just to stay, and most will try to find a way to keep you. Here's that basic script again:

> *'Hi there, my name is [Robert De Niro/Insert Your Name Here]. I've been a loyal customer of yours for _______ years and I'd like to stay on, but I've just received a really good offer from another provider and I think it might be a better deal than the one I'm on. _______ has offered me _______ . I wondered whether you can match it or even beat it? If you can, I'll lock it in right now. Perhaps you could put me through to someone on your retention team to see if they can help?'*

Insider Trick: The De Niro

There's a lot of blind loyalty in health insurance. To use the corporate jargon we looked at in Part 1, a lot of us are 'Sleeping Beauties', peacefully snoring away while our premiums rise year after year.

Only about 5% of policyholders switch health funds each year, compared to about 20–25% of energy bill payers.

Why don't people shop around more? It looks hard! There are hospital and extras policies, they have confusing names, they're hard to compare, and then there's a maze of government rewards and penalties as the cherry on top.

And because it's about your family's health instead of your car or your power bill or your dog, you're more afraid than usual of making a bad call. It really plays into those human traits of 'loss aversion' and 'status quo bias' that I explained in Part 2 of this book.

So the first insider trick you need to get your head around if you want to win the war on this bill is the De Niro. You need to muster the 'cojones' to walk away from your current policy if it's not doing it for you.

The key is to keep it simple. If you were hiring a tradie, would you get a quote from everyone in the Yellow Pages? Of course not. You'd get three quotes and you'll have a good basis for a solid decision.

Health insurance is not so different. Use the Gold, Silver, Bronze and Basic categories and go from there – and don't be afraid to get some free help as there's plenty out there.

True Story: Martin Leaves His Health Fund After 30 Years Of Staying Loyal

One of the best things a One Big Switch member has ever sent us was a letter that Martin Doyle wrote to the CEO of his old health fund when he finally decided to switch after about 30 years. Here it is, reproduced with permission from Martin:

01.05.2015

Dear Sir,

I am writing to you today to express how sad I feel to be leaving.

I have been a loyal member since the early 1980s and in that time have held top cover over the years until very recently when I drew back my cover premium to Basic Hospital and Top Extras.

The final straw for me was your offering to your members for a free annual dental check, but only by an approved provider. I have had the same dentist for a number of years, so it is highly unlikely that I, and I'm certain many members, would change dentist for a free yearly check-up. Ask your partner to change hairdresser or barber for a free annual haircut and I'm sure you will get an appropriate response!

Loyalty is about recognising your members and it's sometimes the small gestures that bind the threads together.

I have now been swayed by One Big Switch. I made a five-minute call yesterday, secured a new policy cover quote which more than equals my current policy cover and I will also be getting a generous cash bonus from making the switch!

A follow-up call today efficiently confirmed all details to switch and begin this relationship.

I am sorry to be parting ways, having invested so many years with you. However I now look forward to moving to a provider that was actually prepared to fight for my business and am looking forward to that new relationship.

Best regards,
Martin Doyle

P.S. I hope this letter actually reaches your desk.

Insider Trick: Under-the-Table Deals

There's not a lot of discounting in this industry. In fact, there's a government-regulated cap on discounts of 12%! (Thanks for nothing, Canberra . . .)

But one of the best-kept secrets in health insurance is a handy little lurk known as 'contribution group discounts'.

There's a weird little loophole in the law that allows health funds to create groups of people and give them all an ongoing discount up to that 12% cap.

That means 'contribution group' members can save up to $480 on a typical $4000 family premium! Although most of the discounts seem to fall into the 4–8% range.

It was created many, many years ago to allow company-wide corporate discounts and that sort of thing, but these days it's being used by everyone from uni staff to government employees to motoring clubs and consumer clubs.

If your fund has a contribution group available to your workplace or a club you belong to (or maybe just to anyone who asks), see if they'll put you in it. It never hurts to ask.

Here are some examples of recent contribution group offers and other under-the-table deals I've seen from motoring clubs and group discount clubs:

NSW: 7.5% discount for NRMA members with Australian Unity
WA: $400 cashback for RAC WA members with HCF
SA: 5% discount for RAA members with HCF
NATIONAL: Up to $300 cashback for One Big Switch members with HCF
NATIONAL: Up to $800 cashback over 2 years for 9Saver members with AIA Health

AVOID BIG GAP PAYMENTS

Potential saving: $1000s

It's the #1 most irritating thing about health insurance, even worse than the ever-rising premiums. It's gaps!

You pay your premium month after month, you hardly ever claim, and then when you do . . . there's still a bloody great out-of-pocket payment. These average over $300 but can be thousands for certain procedures.

The gap is the difference between what the health fund covers and what the specialist or hospital charges. You may not be able to avoid them altogether but you can minimise them by shopping around among hospitals or specialists online. Here's how:

Hospital Fee Gaps: Many hospitals have agreements with health funds to cover gaps entirely or partially (on top of any exact excess or co-payment you've agreed to pay when you took out your policy).

Check which hospitals have a deal with your fund on the federal government website before you decide where to have a procedure: www.privatehealth.gov.au/dynamic/agreementhospitals.aspx

Medical Fee Gaps or Doctors' Fee Gaps: Some doctors also have agreements with certain funds to cover some or all gaps. It could be a 'no gap' deal or a 'known gap' deal, which caps the gap at a certain amount.

Check which doctors have a deal with your fund at the government website before you pick a specialist: www.privatehealth.gov.au/dynamic/gapdoctors.aspx

If your fund does *not* have a deal with the hospital and/or doctor you are planning to use, you have three options:

1. Change hospitals (your doctor might be prepared to do this);
2. Change doctors (your GP or health fund might recommend another specialist); or
3. Change funds (but make sure you won't have to serve any new waiting periods for your procedure).

Shop around for specialists: Most of us simply use the specialist recommended by our GP, but what if they just chose them because they play golf together on the weekends or went to university together?

Technology is now making it easier to compare the prices and performance of specialists too.

New 'Doctor Review' websites such as HealthShare.com.au and Whitecoat.com.au are displaying more info about specialists' fees and patient ratings to make it easier for others to choose their own specialist if they want to.

Health funds such as NIB, HBF and HCF also have agreements with these websites to give their members access to extra information – so ask them about it.

The federal government has also created a 'Medical Costs Finder' website so you can see what the typical gap payments are for certain procedures in different states (it might work out hundreds of dollars cheaper for you to have your surgery done across the border ...). Google 'Medical Costs Finder' to see what info they have.

As journalist Bek Day's story below shows, shopping around for a cheaper specialist could save you as much as $4000 on a single operation.

True Story: Bek Saves $8000 Over Two Years With Health Insurance Savings Hacks

I told you earlier about my friend and colleague Bek Day, who's made a bit of a name for herself finding health insurance savings hacks and publishing them where she works at Kidspot.com.au and News.com.au. I'll let her explain to you how she did it:

'I would conservatively say I have saved about $8000 on my health insurance in two years by customising and streamlining my policy and shopping around for medical practitioners who offer a service.

'One occasion was when my husband needed an operation on his nose. We were facing a $4500 out-of-pocket cost, and with research I managed to avoid paying anything.

'When I spoke to our fund, they explained it was because the specialist was charging five times the Medicare Schedule Fee. They told me about a website called HealthShare, where you can search for a doctor in your area who performs the procedure you need with either no gap (no out-of-pocket expenses) or a 'known gap' (a maximum of $500).

'Within a week we saw a doctor in our area, told him the other quote was far too expensive, and he agreed to do the surgery for a 'known gap' of $500.

'Another really simple one is to find out what your hospital excess is. When I phoned up to enquire about how I could save on my policy, I was informed that by increasing my excess to $500, I would save $50 per month on my policy. This means a saving of $600 a year, for only a $50 increase in the excess – which I only need to pay if I go to

hospital. So far, touch wood, I haven't needed hospitalisation, which means in the two years since discovering this, I've saved our family $1200.

'There are all sorts of ways you can reduce the costs associated with your private health insurance, not only when you need a procedure, but on your monthly premiums as well. A lot of people don't know about this – or, perhaps, don't know where to start – which is why I'm so passionate about educating people on the topic.'

Insider Trick: David's Slingshot

This is the name I give to the kitbag of internet tools that are making us more powerful as consumers than we've ever been before.

The internet is your saviour when it comes to tackling a big health insurance bill, so get online. If computers just aren't your thing, that's OK – invite someone around who is computer-literate and point them at the keyboard!

There are three main Slingshots you can use to save on this:

Slingshot #1: Commercial comparison websites. They don't contain ALL health funds but they're very good at what they do.

This was one of the first household bills to spawn commercial comparison websites because they could see it was getting more expensive, it was confusing, and people needed help.

So whether it's CompareClub.com.au or Comparethemarket.com.au or another one, use them! They all know their stuff, it's a free service as long as you're willing to give your number, and while you *will* have to spend some time on the phone with them (they'll only show you plans once you've given them your phone number), you'd be brave to try and tackle this bill solo.

Here's the thing, though. You *don't* have to buy through them. You should use them as a research tool, ask them to email you their results, and only buy through them if they present the best option.

Also, check out OneBigSwitch.com.au – we're a little different because we tend to have special offers with one or two providers at a time rather than a broader range of on-market deals. But because we have over 1.3 million households as members, we're able to negotiate some outstanding deals.

Slingshot #2: Use the government website PrivateHealth.gov.au (but DON'T SAY I DIDN'T WARN YOU!)

It was American ratbag writer PJ O'Rourke who said, 'Giving money and power to government is like giving whiskey and car keys to teenage boys.'

This website is the technological equivalent of a drunken car crash. It's very clunky and hard to use.

But it *does* claim to show every plan on the market and it does help you see what category each plan falls into. It also has some data on the various funds such as what they pay out, how many complaints they get and so on. If you're determined to dig deeper and deeper, there is a page on the website for each fund with a tab that shows their 'Performance', including how much they return to members ('Benefits as a percentage of contributions') and their 'Member retention' percentage: go to www.privatehealth.gov.au/dynamic/insurer. So you can use it if you need any of that info, but again: don't say I didn't warn you.

FAQs

Doesn't Medicare already provide free health insurance for everybody?

Sort of. Medicare and the public health system cover a lot of health treatments, such as GP visits, emergency departments and public hospital procedures.

We have a universal, free public hospital system and Medicare is one of the best healthcare systems in the world.

But it doesn't cover the following, so if this sounds like you, you'll have to consider private cover:

- You want to choose your own doctor for any elective surgery or hospital visits;
- You want your own room if you have to go to hospital;

- You want to choose which hospital you go to for elective surgery;
- You want a procedure which is 'not clinically necessary' such as cosmetic surgery;
- You want to choose your own dentist;
- You want ambulance cover in certain states; and/or
- You want cover for 'allied health services' such as dental, physio, optometry or podiatry.

More info here: www.privatehealth.gov.au/healthinsurance/what iscovered/

What does health insurance NOT cover?

There are two types of policy: Hospital cover and 'Extras' cover. The hospital policy covers you for treatment as a private patient in a private or public hospital – it helps cover the cost of in-hospital treatment by a doctor of your choice, accommodation in hospital and theatre fees for surgery. But it does not cover visits to the GP or to many other specialists OUTSIDE of hospital. For example, let's say you're having a baby – your health insurance won't cover the visits to your obstetrician before the birth but it might cover your stay in hospital and specialist fees for the birth.

The extras policy covers 'allied health services' outside hospital such as dentists, optometrists and physiotherapists. But since April 2019 it no longer covers many alternative therapies such as aromatherapy, homeopathy and iridology.

PRO TIP

If you've got health insurance, you may never have to pay for sunglasses again! Here's why. If you have any sort of prescription, even 19:20 vision, you can claim for a pair of prescription sunglasses on most extras policies.

So get a free eye check (it's covered by Medicare), and if the optometrist prescribes any sort of eyeglasses, no matter how subtle, you'll probably be able to order prescription sunglasses and claim them on your extras policy.

I have an annual limit of around $200 for optometry, so every other year I get a new pair of sunnies. No gap!

Do I need private health insurance?

Nobody 'needs' private health cover as such, but you have to make your own call about whether you want it. There are three things to consider here: your health, your tax status, and your general attitude to risk.

Firstly, if any of the health matters listed above are quite important to you, then you might want some private health insurance. Or you might have a particular condition that pretty much requires it.

Secondly, for some people the tax system makes it just as expensive *not* to have cover, because you pay extra tax if you don't have a hospital policy (more detail on that below). If that's you, you might as well take out private cover.

Thirdly, you need to decide if you're someone who is prepared to pay for total peace of mind, or would rather play the odds and save the cash (or put it in a bank account and 'self-insure' in case anything major happens). That one's a very personal decision, and it's a decision you need to make with all of your insurances.

Why do the premiums keep going up?

We have an ageing population and the cost of medical procedures is rising fast. Since the Baby Boomers started getting older and claiming more on their policies, premiums have gone up for over 20 years in a row. According to CHOICE's quarterly polling, this became one of the top two most stressful bills for Aussie households.

How do the government penalties and incentives work?

The federal government has bankrolled this industry to the tune of around $7 billion a year in rebates to take some pressure off the public health system.

Millions of us are more or less forced to take out a policy by a convoluted hodgepodge of 'sticks and carrots' in the tax system. So we have to get our heads around these rules.

Carrot: The 'Private Health Insurance Rebate' means the government covers up to 33% of your premium, depending on your age and income.

Stick: The 'Lifetime Health Cover Loading' means that if you don't take out cover by the year you turn 31, you'll pay an extra 2% premium for every year you put it off. (For example, leave it until you're 40 and you'll pay an extra 20% if you want to take out cover.)

Stick: The Medicare Levy we pay at tax time goes *up* if you don't have a private hospital insurance policy and you earn above a certain income (currently $90,000 for a single or $180,000 for a household).

Carrot: Discounts for younger people. Take out private health insurance between the ages of 18 and 29 and you'll get a 2% discount for every year you're under 30, up to a maximum of 10% (for example, take it out at 25 and you'll get a 10% discount).

Do I need private health insurance to get ambulance cover?

In some states, you might. It all depends where you live. The government website summarises it well in the table below:

State	Ambulance Cover arrangements in your state of residence
All states and territories	Department of Veterans Affairs Gold Card holders are covered for state ambulance services in every state by the Department.
ACT	Health Care Concession Card and Pensioner Concession Card holders are entitled to free emergency ambulance services. If you are not eligible for a concession and want to be covered, you can purchase insurance from a private health fund.

State	Ambulance Cover arrangements in your state of residence
NSW	Health Care Concession Card, Pensioner Concession Card, and Commonwealth Seniors Health Card holders are entitled to free ambulance transport services. If you are not eligible for a concession and want to be covered, you can purchase insurance from a private health fund.
NT	Pensioner Concession Card and Commonwealth Seniors Health Card holders are entitled to free ambulance transport services. If you are not eligible for a concession and want to be covered, you can purchase insurance from a private health fund or a subscription through the state ambulance service.
QLD	Ambulance costs for Queensland residents are covered by the state government.
SA	If you want ambulance cover you can purchase insurance from a private health fund or a subscription through the state ambulance service.
TAS	Ambulance costs for Tasmanian residents are covered by the state government.
VIC	Pensioner Concession Card and Healthcare Card holders are entitled to free ambulance transport services. If you are not eligible for a concession and want to be covered, you can purchase insurance from a private health fund or a subscription through the state ambulance service.
WA	Aged Pensioner concession holders are entitled to free ambulance transport services. If you are not eligible for a concession and want to be covered, you can purchase insurance from a private health fund or a subscription through the state ambulance service.

Source: www.privatehealth.gov.au.

What if I've got a pre-existing condition?

Pre-existing conditions stop a lot of people from switching or taking up health insurance because they assume they can't. The truth is, pre-existing conditions *do* make it more complex, but it's not impossible. Here's what the ombudsman says: 'A health insurer may impose a 12-month waiting period on benefits for hospital treatment for pre-existing conditions . . . Once a member has been on their hospital policy for a continuous period of 12 months, the pre-existing condition waiting period no longer applies and the member is entitled to the full benefits under their policy.' (NB: If you've served this waiting period with one insurer, you don't have to serve it again with another, if you switch to 'comparable cover'. Just be upfront and ask the fund you want to move to whether there's any extra waiting periods and you should be fine.)

Insider Trick: The Squeaky Wheel

If you've got a beef with your health fund, there's help at hand.

Remember the three steps to a successful whinge from Part 1? First, whinge to the boss. If that fails, whinge in public. And finally, whinge to a regulator.

The regulator in this case is called the Commonwealth Ombudsman.

NB: if your beef is with a hospital or a doctor, chances are you need to speak to the health care complaints body in your state or territory. But if it's with your health fund, the ombudsman is the place to go.

The service is free and they're independent and impartial – which means they're not on anyone's side, including yours. 'We do not represent consumers, insurers, hospitals or health services,' they say on their website at www.ombudsman.gov.au/how-we-can-help/private-health-insurance.

CHAPTER 19
CREDIT CARDS

> 'Annual income twenty pounds, annual expenditure nineteen six, result happiness. Annual income twenty pounds, annual expenditure twenty pound ought and six, result misery.'
> ***David Copperfield*, Charles Dickens**

They say ex-smokers are the most pig-headed critics of smoking and that's me when it comes to credit cards, I'm afraid.

For years, I had around $3000 of debt on a credit card I'd applied for in my 20s - about the national average at the time - and for years I paid hundreds of dollars in interest for the privilege of spending other people's money.

But then my better half talked me into paying it off and chopping it up, and I learnt how the credit card industry really works.

So now I'm not a fan. In fact, I'd go so far as to say I think they're a bit of a hoax.

Essentially, most credit cards are a high-interest loan, averaging almost 20% per annum, dressed up as a status symbol. Ingenious marketing brains have applied lipstick to this pig and made us believe that it's somehow a sign of wealth and sophistication, a rite of passage and a passport to rare privileges.

What's really dastardly about the cards is that they're designed to punish the financially illiterate - like 25-year-old me - and use that profit to reward the financially-savvy (like 45-year-old me).

If you pay your card off every month and spend a lot of money on it and earn a lot of points, good luck to you. But half of card users don't. And they need to know they're funding your free bubbles and foot massages in the business class lounge.

If you want to know how they talk about you behind closed doors at your credit card company, read on.

If not, skip to the next chapter.

INSIDE INFO

You know those people who like to say 'there are two types of people'? Well, the people who work in the credit card industry are those people.

In their eyes, you're either a 'revolver' or a 'transactor'.

If you spend a small fortune on your credit card through your business (or your family) and you pay the balance off each month, then you might be amassing thousands of reward points and paying no interest, in which case you're a winner.

To credit card insiders, you're what's called a 'transactor', and frankly you're not much use to them.

But if, like around half of Australians, you've constantly got a few grand on the card and you're always paying interest, you're what's called a 'revolver', my friend. And you're their ideal customer.

It might sound kind of sexy, but revolvers are the mugs of the credit card world. They're the reason banks and other lenders make billions from the not-so-fantastic plastic, and how they pay for points and rewards schemes, free insurance and other perks.

If revolvers were to crunch the numbers and work out what they pay the credit card provider and what they get back, they'd come out behind.

In a nutshell

Potential saving	Around $600/year
Easiest	'The balance transfer hack'
Next-easiest	'The fundamentals'
Top tools	Comparison sites
If I could tell you one thing about credit card bills it would be:	This is one bill that's not necessary

THE BALANCE TRANSFER HACK

Potential saving: Around $600/year

The easiest way to save on credit card bills is to pay them off and never have to think about them again. Simple as that. #sorrynotsorry

And the easiest way to pay them off is using the 'balance transfer hack'.

Here's a four-step guide, but it *only* works if you use it to pay the balance down.

1. **Go to Finder.com.au or Canstar.com.au and search for 'Balance Transfer Cards'.** Look for a card with a long balance transfer period. In some cases, you can pay 0% interest for about three years on the balance you move from another card! Ideally, pick one that also has a low or *no* annual fee and a low or *no* 'balance transfer fee'.
2. **Divide your balance by the number of months the balance transfer will last (e.g. $3000 divided by 36 = $83.33/month).** You're going to set up a regular transfer from your monthly pay to cover the amount. In fact, add $5 just so there are no nasty surprises at the end. (Got too much debt? No way you can cover it in that time frame? I'd suggest you call the National Debt Help

Hotline on 1800 007 007 or go to FinancialCounsellingAustralia.org.au and ask for their help.)

3. **Apply to move your credit card balance to the new balance transfer card.** Move any direct debits you have set up onto your transaction account or a debit card. Close the old credit card. Chop it up!
4. **Now put the new card in a tray of water and pop it in the freezer, thereby encasing it in ice like Han Solo in *The Empire Strikes Back*.** You are going to try to never use this card. It'll be there for emergencies, but you'll have to wait for it to thaw while you take a good long hard look at yourself!

Insider Trick: The Elizabeth Taylor

If you're cunning, you might have read the 'Balance Transfer Hack' above and thought, 'I could just do that over and over again and enjoy interest honeymoon after interest honeymoon, Liz Taylor-style.'

And you'd be right. It is possible to go from balance transfer offer to balance transfer offer, and some people do.

BUT there are pitfalls in this strategy. The Liz Taylor can be a dangerous trick when dealing with credit products, because repeated applications for new loans can leave your credit report looking like something the dog ate, and then brought back up, and then ate again.

Your credit report or credit score is often described as your financial CV: lenders use it when deciding whether to lend to you. So if you make a lot of applications for credit in a short period of time, it's there for anyone to see for up to 5 years and they may count it against you when assessing an application.

According to Credit Savvy, 'When you apply for a credit product, a credit enquiry is recorded on your credit file by the credit provider. How enquiries affect your credit score depends on the frequency and recentness of the enquiries, the type of credit applied for and the provider of the credit. These are recorded on your file for five years.'

Since 2018, Australia has also had 'Comprehensive Credit Reporting', which means lenders can see even more of your good and bad credit activity. If you're someone who makes all your repayments, that's a good thing. But if not, you're now even more exposed than before.

THE FUNDAMENTALS

Potential saving: Around $300/year

Simply understanding how credit cards work and getting the fundamentals right can also save you hundreds of relatively easy dollars. Here's what everyone with a credit card needs to know:

Pay the balance off every month or pay a double price: Your card might say you get '55 days interest free on purchases', but here's the catch: if you don't pay it off each month, that interest holiday gets reversed, and you pay interest on ALL your purchases.

There are some very low-rate credit cards that aren't widely advertised: There are plenty of cards with rates under 10% and low (or no) annual fees. They won't have all the bells and whistles of rewards cards, but check for yourself: how many rewards are you *really* getting for your high interest rate and big annual fee? Most comparison sites do not display these cheap-as-chips credit cards (the card providers make so little money off them that they usually don't pay others commission for selling them – which is exactly what you're looking for!).

NUMBER CRUNCH

Thanks to a global pandemic and the growth of interest-free Buy Now Pay Later alternatives, Aussies are finally wising up about the credit card trap.

2017 was the height of our plastic addiction: we had over 17 million credit cards nationally and the corporate watchdog reported that:

- We had a combined balance of $45 billion on our cards.
- We were paying $445 million a year in interest and $1.5 billion in fees.
- About one in two Aussies had a card.
- One in three of those had more than one card.
- One in 20 even had more than five credit cards!

But since then, we've reduced the number of cards to around 13 million and the debt to less than half – around $18 billion in mid-2022. We've almost paid down our debt to the level it was at 20 years ago.

Debit cards are now the #1 way to pay for stuff down under. Aussie Aussie Aussie!

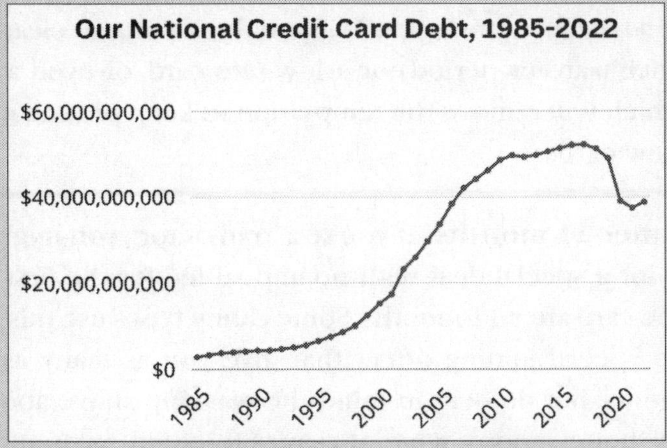

Source: Reserve Bank of Australia

Never pay the 'minimum repayment' if you can afford to pay more: The minimum repayment varies but it's normally around 3% of what you owe. Pay that each month and it'll only take you about 60 LONG YEARS to be debt-free (and that's assuming you don't put more on the card). So you should always pay more than the minimum repayment. Pay the lot if you can.

Don't take out cash advances: When you take cash off your plastic, you pay interest (often about 20% per annum) from the day you do so, and you also pay a cash advance fee. Double whammy!

Don't blindly accept whatever credit limit they offer you: The bank will decide what limit they want to offer you. So what? Since when did they know what's best for you? Decide for yourself. What's the maximum you're prepared to owe them? Set that as your limit. They're no longer allowed to offer you increases without you asking for them – unless you give them permission to do so. If you don't want to be offered credit limit increases, tell them that's your preference.

Consolidate your credit cards: If you've got multiple cards with balances on them, why not move all that debt into one place with as low an interest rate as possible, and then pay it down? It could be a balance transfer card (if you think you can clear it during the balance transfer period) or a low-rate card, or even a personal loan – which will remove the temptation to keep putting more debt on the new card.

Cancel after 11 months: If you're a 'transactor', you might be able to apply for a special deal with no annual fee for the first year and cancel the card after 11 months. Some canny types use this loophole to access special joining offers that give you as many as 100,000 bonus points. But do bear in mind the warning above about taking too many 'honeymoons' when it comes to credit cards and loans: it can sometimes hurt your credit score.

Insider Trick: David's Slingshot

Good news! Credit cards are up there with telco products for the easiest bills to compare online. The internet really has made it a piece of cake to find a cheaper card.

In fact, some of the biggest comparison websites started out only doing credit cards because they were so easy to compare online. (Finder.com.au is now the most-visited comparison website in Australia, covering more than a dozen different household bills, but it started out as CreditCardFinder.com.au.)

This means you can find and apply for a cheaper card in the time it takes to drink a cup of tea or coffee, if you know what you're looking for.

You'll just need to decide first of all whether you're a 'revolver' or a 'transactor' (be honest with yourself), and therefore whether you need a low rate or balance transfer card (for revolvers) or a rewards or gold or platinum card (strictly for transactors).

Which type of card is right for me?

We might aspire to being the jetsetter with a platinum credit card, gold frequent flyer status and a boarding pass for Seat 1A (all posted to Instagram with the hashtag #winning, of course). But if that really is you, you're probably reading the wrong book!

Most of us are down the back end of the plane (if we're even on it), among the screaming kids, the mouth-breathers and the banging toilet door. Because that's where all the real fun happens! And we should choose the card to match. The first step on the road to credit card savings is: *be realistic*.

Cards are like cars – you wouldn't buy a Porsche SUV if you can't afford the upfront cost, the fuel bill and the expensive European parts. So don't apply for the Porsche of credit cards if you're a Hyundai driver. (Like me! Nothing wrong with Hyundai drivers.)

Here's a rundown of the different types of card, who they're best for, and what type of car they'd be if you were buying one of those instead.

CREDIT CARD	IF IT WAS A CAR . . .	GOOD FOR	PROS	CONS
Low rate cards	**Trusty five-year-old Toyota Corolla**	'Revolvers': People who are unable to repay their credit card debt in full at the end of each month – as the interest charged is minimal.	Simplicity and price; they often have an annual fee of $100 or less and rates can be less than 10% p.a.	No complimentary perks and benefits such as frequent flyer points, free insurance and access to airport lounges; but you can still sometimes get a balance transfer deal, giving you 6–24 months of 0% interest to pay your debt down.
Reward point cards	**New Mazda or Volkswagen**	'Transactors': People who spend a lot on their credit card and pay it off each month.	Joining offers can feature up to 100,000 points, and you can earn points from all your everyday spending and bills.	Often have a higher annual fee and/or a reward programme fee, and a higher interest rate. Check the fees don't outweigh the rewards! It will come down to how much you spend on the card.

CREDIT CARD	IF IT WAS A CAR . . .	GOOD FOR	PROS	CONS
Balance transfer cards	**Silver Service Taxi**	'Revolvers' or 'Transactors': Anyone who wants to minimise credit card costs for a limited period of time.	People who want to consolidate debt and pay it down over a set period of time.	There is sometimes a fee of around 2% of your balance, and they usually revert to a high rate. Taking offer after offer can also hurt your credit score (see above).
Gold and platinum cards	**Porsche SUV**	Travelling 'Transactors': People who spend a lot, travel a lot and can afford the higher fees and interest rates.	Common benefits include bonus points, lounge passes at airports, and complimentary insurances such as purchase protection, travel insurance or car hire excess insurance.	A much higher annual fee (e.g. $500) and interest rate (e.g. up to 25% p.a.). Also, higher minimum credit limits (e.g. $15,000) so you need to be disciplined about keeping the balance down.

Insider Trick: The Red Dog

There are websites devoted to getting the most out of credit card joining offers and reward schemes. The best-known of these is called 'Point Hacks', and there's also 'I Fly Flat'.

In fact there's a whole thriving subculture out there of people who play the credit card rewards game like it's high-stakes poker. These people have been reading this chapter and shouting at the book, 'No! You fool! This guy has no idea what he's on about!'

Like most gamblers, 'point hackers' like to tell you about their wins and some have been known to rack up enough points to fly First Class just by amassing special offers and exploiting various tricks and loopholes.

They do exist. Some of them are among my closest friends. If you can pull it off, then more power to you.

But I've largely left it out of this book because strictly speaking, it's not a money-saving strategy per se. It's more a reward-maximisation strategy. It also involves spending quite a lot, albeit while ensuring you get maximum payback for your spend.

Are rewards schemes worth it?

This one is up there with 'What's the meaning of life?' and 'Why did God invent mosquitoes?'. It's the $64,000 question when it comes to credit cards, and it's very hard to answer.

In fact, the answer is constantly changing because the value of a rewards point is constantly changing.

In mid-2018, the value of points was cut because of some new 'interchange fee' rules that the government brought in, so for many of us the answer to this question is now 'yeah, nah, not really'.

NUMBER CRUNCH

A Qantas Frequent Flyer point is worth about 1.8c on average, according to Point Hacks. In March 2019, RateCity looked at the worst big bank cards for redeeming products through the Qantas store and found that to get a $200 SMEG kettle, you needed to spend:
$133,470 on ANZ Frequent Flyer
$77,860 on Westpac's Altitude Qantas
$74,520 on NAB Qantas Rewards
$51,900 on Commbank Awards

After extensive research I've come to the conclusion that most rewards schemes are designed to be confusing. This is because the points are not worth much in real dollar value, so the goal of the points scheme architect is to make you believe they're worth more than they really are. In fact, you could go so far as to say that's the job of marketers throughout history – to create a 'perceived value' that is higher than a product's intrinsic value. So, with rewards schemes, there's a lot of talk about status and 'bonus points' and holidays and shopping on their websites, but not much about the actual, no-BS dollar value of their points. If you're not a big spender, and you're not into numbers, consider dumping the rewards card if it's costing you anything in the form of card fees or higher interest – and skipping the rest of this chapter.

Still here? OK then, let's delve a bit deeper into this question of whether points are worthwhile.

As a basic rule, you need to see what the cost of accessing the rewards scheme is, and compare that to the value of the rewards you get over a year.

If 'Cost of Rewards' > 'Value of Rewards', it's not worth it, and vice versa.

The cost of access is the easy bit: it will usually be an annual fee on the card, and these can range up to $500.

There might also be a cost to join a rewards program such as Qantas Frequent Flyer if you're not already a member. In some cases it will be the extra cost you pay to be with a more expensive provider such as Telstra or Westpac.

Another cost of access is the higher interest rate on rewards cards, averaging about 20% p.a. (Although if you pay the card off each month, you can ignore this one.)

As for the value of rewards, this is where it gets tricky. Working this out can make your brain ache. But here's one (relatively) simple way to do it:

1. Estimate your weekly spend on the card (look at a statement), then multiply that by 52 weeks to get your estimated annual spend.
2. Work out how many reward points you'll earn over the year. (E.g. Two points per dollar spent means you multiply the annual spend by two, and so on.)
3. Now that you know roughly how many points you'll earn in a year, you can go to the website of the relevant reward scheme and see how many gift cards your annual points balance would buy (I just checked mine and 55,000 points only gets me about $250 of gift cards, for example).
4. Or, you can use a 'points calculator' like the one below to see what your annual points would buy you in frequent flyer points, and you can use the usual cost of those flights to estimate the value.

'Point Hacks' Points Calculator: www.pointhacks.com.au/community/tools-calculators/credit-card-reward-program-conversion-calculator/

Are you still here? OK, well this is where this chapter enters the Twilight Zone. If you make it to the end of the next part, pour yourself a tall glass of something nice because you'll have trekked right into the dark heart of the credit card rewards jungle and returned to tell the tale.

At financial comparison website Canstar.com.au, they've bravely attempted to create a mathematical equation to calculate whether you're better off with or without a particular rewards credit card. They call it 'Net Reward Return' and it looks like this:

$$\frac{\text{POINTS EARNED IN A YEAR}}{\text{POINTS REQUIRED TO REDEEM \$1 OF REWARD}} = \text{REWARD RETURN}$$

So let's say you spend $24,000 a year on your card and earn 24,000 points, and your rewards scheme requires 150 points to redeem $1 of value on a gift card or other reward.

Canstar reports that your equation will look something like this:

$$\frac{\$24\text{k} = 24{,}000 \text{ points}}{150 \text{ points} / \$1} = \$160$$

Because your 'Net Reward Return' comes out at $160, you'll be better off with this card if your annual fees and costs for having the card are *under* $160. You'll be worse off if they're over that amount.

Get it? I did warn you . . .

CHAPTER 20
PETROL

'I'm sure that in 1985, plutonium *is* available at every corner drugstore, but in 1955 it's a little hard to come by.'
Doc, *Back To The Future*

We're going to deal with petrol and groceries next, which are a different category of bill to utilities, insurance and credit cards.

With those other bills, you can stage a once-a-year 'bill-itzkrieg', give yourself a pat on the backside and you're the winner for another 12 months.

But with these ones, it's more of a war of attrition. This is the western front of the household budget.

Petrol prices briefly dropped below $1 during the COVID-19 pandemic. Shame most of us weren't driving anywhere much!

Ever since, though, they've been a nightmare for drivers, skyrocketing to over $2.10 when the war in Ukraine began. This ACCC graph tells the sorry story:

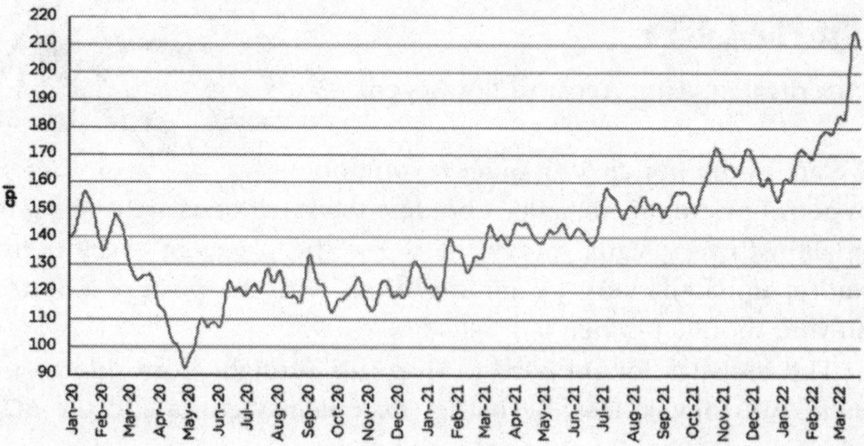

Source: ACCC © Commonwealth of Australia

A cut in fuel excise tax brought them under $2 again in 2022, but it was only temporary.

Many Aussies commute long distances, so this is a big bill when prices are that high – over $5000 a year for some families. But there's plenty of easy money to be saved if you adopt a few key habits that can save a household thousands of dollars over time.

As always, we're gonna start with the easiest hacks and go from there.

In a nutshell

Potential saving	Up to $40 a tank or $2000/year
Easiest	'Fuel price apps' and 'Picking the cycle'
Next-easiest	'Discount schemes' and 'The basics'
Top tools	Petrol Spy and Ruckus Energy
If I could tell you one thing about petrol bills it would be:	Check your phone before you pull in to fill up – but not while you're driving!

FUEL PRICE APPS

Potential saving: Around $600/year

We are in the middle of a quiet revolution in petrol pricing in Australia – but less than half of us are cashing in. In almost every state, you can now see the prices of every petrol station, updated every 15 minutes or so, with the push of a button on your mobile phone.

The industry fought hard to stop this sunlight from shining on them, but they've lost the battle (except in Victoria and the ACT, which are still holding out as I write this).

This transparency gives you a power you've never had before. Think about it – just about every other provider of a household bill advertises their prices online, where they can be found and compared easily – from energy to telco, insurance and even groceries.

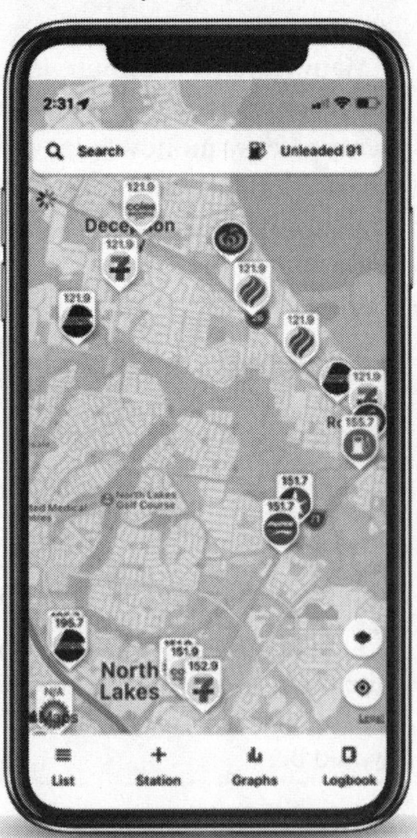

But until recently, the only way to know what a petrol station was charging was to drive right up to it and check the 3-metre sign out front. By the time you'd done that, what was the point of going anywhere else? And that was just how they liked it – their profits basically came down to location, location, location, and competition just meant keeping an eye on the signs across the road.

But now, you can check a fuel price app before pulling out of your driveway and sometimes find a 50c/L difference between two stations on your drive to work. That's a $40 saving when filling up a Toyota Hilux, or a $25 difference on a Corolla.

In fact, in this screenshot from August 2022, there was 74c/L difference between nearby stations in Brisbane.

NUMBER CRUNCH

In 2020, Griffith University estimated 1 in 5 drivers were using petrol price apps. By now it should be much higher, but maybe not a majority of us yet.

Even before the recent spike in fuel prices, the ACCC reckoned that these apps could save motorists $275 million a year, including:
$340/year for Sydney drivers,
$150 for Melbourne,
$230 for Brisbane,
$210 in Perth, and
$160 in Adelaide.

Insider Trick: David's Slingshot

Technology is finally breaking down the barriers to comparing prices.

If you're in NSW, WA, Tasmania and the NT, your state/territory government has forced petrol stations to report their prices several times a day to a government fuel app or website.

In QLD and SA, they've mandated for petrol stations to give their information to app developers.

In Victoria and the ACT, apps do their best to pull together a mix of publicly-available and crowd-sourced info.

And there are national apps that use a mixture of all of the above. Here are some of the best (I've only included free ones) . . .

STATE-BASED APPS:

FuelCheck NSW

Made by:	NSW Government
Where to get it:	App Store, Google Play, FuelCheck.nsw.gov.au
Fuel types:	11, including EV charging stations
Includes:	Price trends and averages
Covers:	Metro and most regional areas

FuelWatch website/email service (WA)

Made by:	WA Government
Where to get it:	FuelWatch.wa.gov.au
Fuel types:	7
Includes:	Today's price and tomorrow's price, plus price history and trends
Covers:	Metro and most regional areas

RACQ Fair Fuel Finder app (QLD)

Made by:	RACQ
Where to get it:	App Store, Google Play, RACQ.com.au
Fuel types:	6
Includes:	Price trends and averages, plus a 'fair fuel price' for each area

RACV website (VIC)

Made by:	RACV
Where to get it:	RACV.com.au
Fuel types:	14
Includes:	Price trends and averages
Covers:	Metro and regional areas

RAA (SA)

Made by:	RAA
Where to get it:	RAA.com.au
Fuel types:	7
Covers:	Metro and regional areas

MyFuel NT website

Made by:	NT Government
Where to get it:	MyFuelNT.nt.gov.au
Fuel types:	10
Includes:	Price trends and averages
Covers:	Metro and most regional areas

FuelCheck TAS app (Tas)

Made by:	Tasmanian Government
Where to get it:	App Store, Google Play, FuelCheck.tas.gov.au
Fuel types:	16
Includes:	Price trends and averages
Covers:	Metro and most regional areas

NATIONAL APPS:

There are about a dozen national fuel price apps but here are my top three. When it comes to picking a winner, it's mostly about deciding which one you find easiest to read and most useful. Some have offers from petrol stations, some have ads, and most have price trend graphs so you can see where the cycle is up to – so take a look, pick your favourite, and Robert's your father's brother.

I've screenshotted the same area on the same day to give you an idea of how different they look:

Fuel Map Australia

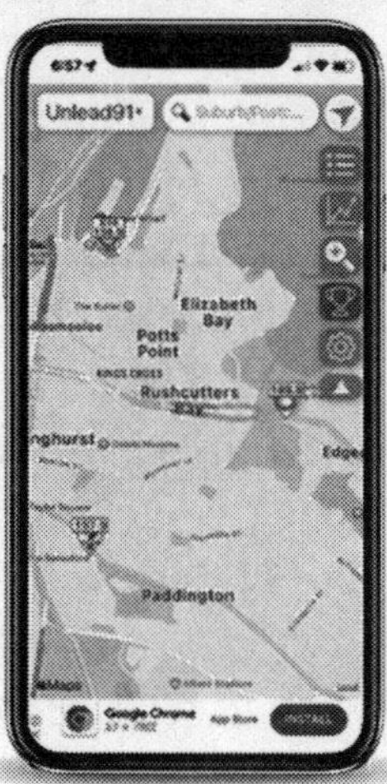

EzySt

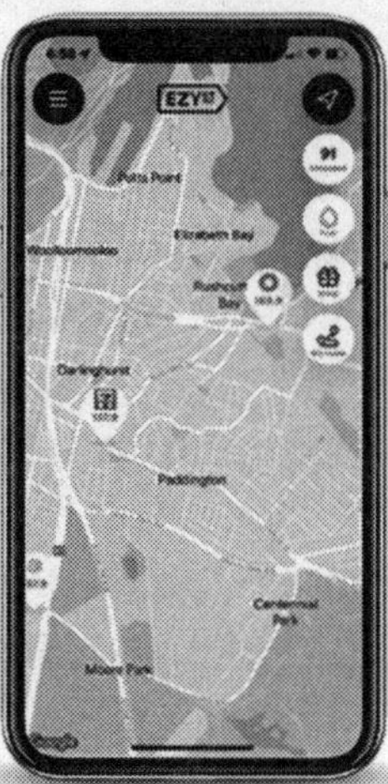

Petrol Spy

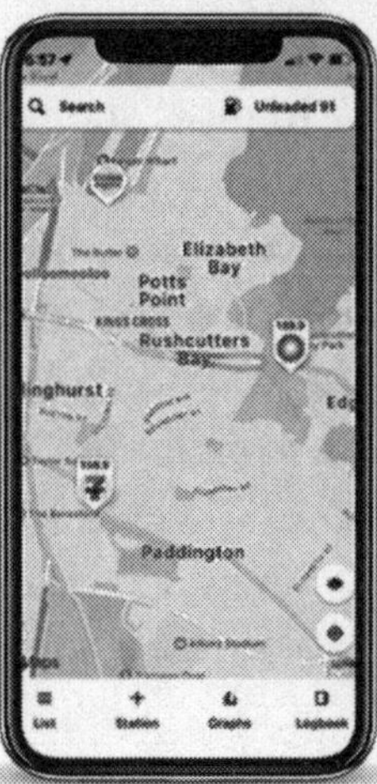

PRO TIP

Consumer group CHOICE compared fuel price apps in May 2022 and found Petrol Spy consistently had the most accurate prices across NSW, the ACT, QLD and VIC.

PICKING THE CYCLE

Potential saving: Around $600/year

There are two 'golden rules' to saving on petrol: fill up at the right place, and fill up at the right time.

Using the apps and sites above will help you find the right place, but they can also help you with timing.

Fuel prices follow an infuriating 'cycle' that goes up and down in an unpredictable way (except in WA).

They 'rise like a rocket and drop like a feather', so filling up a day late can cost you $20 or more per tank if the cycle has spiked.

But fill up at the right time, and, depending on the size of your car and how much you drive, you could save up to 40–50c/L which translates to anywhere from $250 to thousands of dollars a year.

While price cycles *used* to follow a rough weekly pattern, which meant you could just fill up on 'Cheap Tuesdays', they don't anymore (except in WA, where it's *almost always* cheapest every-second Monday and rockets upwards every second Tuesday).

In most states, you've now got to check where the cycle is up to – and once again the key is technology. Most of the apps mentioned above will show you a graph of average petrol prices in your area and give you a recommendation of which days to fill up, so that's one way to check.

You can get the same info on the ACCC website, updated three times a week, at this link:

www.accc.gov.au/consumers/petrol-diesel-lpg/petrol-price-cycles

(Or just google 'ACCC petrol price cycle'.)

In regional areas, you'll find it a lot harder, unfortunately – neither the apps nor the consumer watchdog comprehensively covers price cycles in regional Australia.

NUMBER CRUNCH

The ACCC says: 'Avoiding buying petrol on the 10 days around the price cycle peaks would see motorists save 3.8–6.1 c/L in the capital cities. This would see annual savings of $141 million in Sydney, $124 million in Melbourne, $68 million in Brisbane and $55 million in Adelaide. Our advice for those looking to save even more, say 15–20 c/L, or $9–12 a tank, is to time your purchases.'

DISCOUNT & LOYALTY SCHEMES

Potential saving: Around $500/year

There are a range of discount, loyalty and reward schemes in petrol that can save you money – especially if you're STACKING them with the strategies described above.

If you do pick a loyalty scheme and stick with it, you will save hundreds on your petrol bill compared to someone who just pulls into the next servo each time the fuel light comes on.

You might only have a Coles or a Woolworths fuel outlet nearby, for example, and in that case it pays to pick and stick with one. Or you might do all your shopping at Coles, and have your insurance and credit card with them too – in which case it might make sense for you to buy their fuel. Or you might use the fuel price apps to find the cheapest station and then ALSO use a loyalty discount – which is the Holy Grail of petrol money-savers.

So here's a rundown of the fuel loyalty schemes that exist as of 2022. Note that they're constantly changing, but I've done my best to report the latest versions at the time of print.

There's no 'best' scheme in my view – picking a winner will usually depend on other factors such as where you do your grocery shopping, or which stations are on your commute, or whether you already belong to a motoring club that offers a discount.

Just pick one that works for you and make the most of it.

Insider Trick: The Red Dog

The 'De Niro' trick I described in Part 2 applies to petrol as much as it does to any other bill. Being fiercely disloyal and being prepared to walk (or drive) away when you see a better deal is usually the key to paying as little as possible for your fuel.

But discount and loyalty schemes can save you money - especially if you can use them at stations that are the cheapest on the fuel price apps, and at the bottom of the price cycle.

Just don't fall for the idea that using a loyalty scheme on its own will guarantee you cheap fuel - if the bowser price is 50c/L more than down the road, a 4c/L supermarket shopper docket ain't going to make much difference.

Ruckus Energy

I think this new fuel discount club is the most exciting thing to happen to petrol prices in recent years. At present it's only available in certain NSW locations but it has plans to expand to QLD and Victoria next.

Businesses and governments have been getting 'fleet discounts' on fuel for years but punters have been locked out of them. Basically, Ruckus is a fleet for individual consumers. They buy fuel at wholesale prices and pass on the saving to members.

For a membership fee of $5/month or $50/year, you get bowser prices that average around 15–20c/L less at participating stations. If you fill a typical 50L tank once a week, it works out to about a $390 annual saving for a $50 fee.

Woolworths & Ampol/Caltex

Customers who spend at least $30 at the supermarket earn a discount on fuel. Your supermarket receipts contain a fuel discount offer on the back that is redeemable at all applicable service stations within Australia – and if you have an Everyday Rewards card, it is also stored on the card.

Caltex is gradually re-branding as Ampol in Australia, so participating stations could carry either branding while the transition happens.

You earn one Everyday Rewards point for every dollar you spend at participating outlets.

You can also redeem your 4c/L fuel discount and combine it with another 4c/L offer for spending $5 in-store at the petrol station, making an 8c/L discount overall. (But note that not *all* Ampol/Caltex servos accept the Woolies vouchers.)

Coles & Shell

Like Woolies, customers who spend at least $30 at a Coles supermarket earn a 4c/L discount on fuel. Your supermarket receipts contain a fuel discount offer on the back that is redeemable at all applicable service stations within Australia.

Coles Express allows you to stack 4c/L supermarket vouchers with 4c/L member offers in the Carsales, AFL Live and Linkt toll-road apps in Sydney, Melbourne and Brisbane to make an 8c/L discount. If you spend $20 in-store they'll sometimes give you 14c/L off during promo periods – making for a STACKED discount of up to 22c/L.

With Flybuys you can also earn points on fuel: one point for every $2 spent. Coles has finally moved into the digital age and you can now access your 4c/L discount via the Flybuys app.

Coles, Woolies & Ampol Gift Cards

This is another way to save 3–6% on fuel. You can often get a discount of 4–5% off Coles and Woolworths Gift Cards, some of which can be used to buy petrol. To find these deals, you can look at money-saving websites such as Groupon and OzBargain and The Entertainment Book, or if you're a customer of any of the following companies and clubs they often have them as part of their own rewards programs: RACQ, NRMA, RACV, RAA, RAC, AGL Rewards, Employment Hero and Skoolbag Family Essentials. You can use these in combination with supermarket vouchers and get an effective total discount of around 12c/L off fuel.

You can sometimes get discounts on Ampol gift cards too, at the ShopBack website – usually 3% but occasionally 6%. These can then be combined with the 4c/L supermarket discounts to get an effective total discount of around 10–16c/L off fuel.

Ritchie's IGA

Ritchie's owns about 60 IGA grocery stores on the east coast, most of which have a 4c/L discount with a local fuel station or three.

7-Eleven/Mobil

At 7-Eleven/Mobil they have a fuel app that allows you to lock in a cheap price for seven days if you have one of their fuel cards and you pre-load it. They call it 'fuel price lock'.

True Story

In the early days of the 7-Eleven/Mobil app, some cunning motorists found a loophole where you could turn off your phone's GPS, lie about where you were, and lock in a price from anywhere in the country for a week. By now 7-Eleven/Mobil seems to have caught on to this trick and addressed it in later updates of the app, so this cheap fuel party might be over for the time being.

Motoring Clubs

Motoring Clubs such as the RAC in WA and the RACQ in Queensland have a 4c/L discount with Puma petrol stations. NRMA members in NSW get 3–5c/L off with Ampol. You need to be a member, which costs money, but if you're already a member it's worth checking out.

THE BASICS

Potential saving: Around $500/year

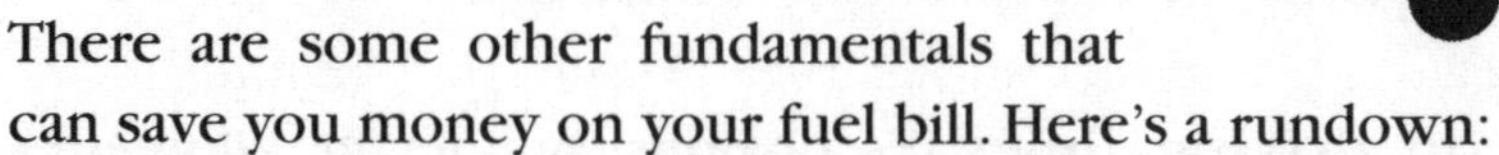

There are some other fundamentals that can save you money on your fuel bill. Here's a rundown:

Go indie: Independent petrol stations are usually cheaper than the majors. A 2020 report by the ACCC found you could save as much as $445 a year by shopping around using the cheapest chains. This table captured the cheapest and most expensive chains by average price in each state/territory.

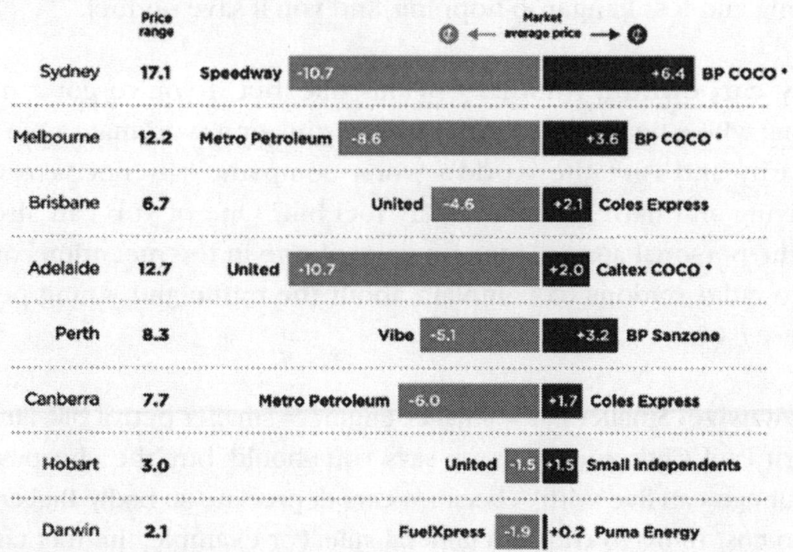

Source: ACCC © Commonwealth of Australia

Buy your petrol at Costco: This one only works if you have a Costco membership (about $60 a year) and you're near a Costco warehouse that sells fuel. But if that's you, Costco fuel is cheap as. In fact, it's consistently the cheapest fuel in Australia!

Cut back on driving time: It's obvious, but fewer kilometres clocked up means more fuel in the tank. Also, a cold engine uses more fuel as it warms up. So take a bus from time to time or ride a bike for short trips, and try to combine your daily errands into one longer journey to really maximise your fuel efficiency.

Avoid peak hour: This is pretty much the secret to everlasting happiness in life, if you ask me. But peak hour is also the worst time to drive for fuel efficiency. You're constantly stopping and starting, braking and accelerating, shifting up and down between the gears, and that sucks up the juice. Your car is most fuel-efficient when it's humming along the motorway at 110 km/h. So do more humming along and less kangaroo-hopping, and you'll save on fuel.

Try carpooling: Another obvious one, but if you've got a neighbour who's heading the same way as you, or a workmate who lives nearby and isn't the world's worst company, why not take turns driving and halve your weekday fuel bill? One of you can also get some personal admin done on your phone in the meantime, or call into radio stations to complain about the traffic and young people these days.

Downsize: Smaller car = smaller engine = smaller petrol bill. Finance guru Paul Clitheroe famously says you should 'buy the cheapest car your ego can live with' – because cars depreciate so badly. Bigger cars also cost more to run, as a general rule. For example, the fuel tank in a Toyota HiLux is almost TWICE the size of the tank in a Corolla. So if you don't have a Hilux-sized ego or you're not a tradie or you're not ferrying 2.5 kids and their associated piles of stuff around, why pay more?

Go easy on the air conditioning: My first car was a 1984 Peugeot 505 with no air con and I used to take it up the coast on long summer roadtrips in 35-degree heat. No problemo! These days I couldn't survive in a car in summer without AC, but it does use extra petrol, so go easy on it if you can.

Pump your tyres up: Inflate your tyres to the maximum recommended pressure (they should have a recommended range written on the side of the tyre somewhere). This can improve fuel consumption by up to 2%, and it also makes your tyres last longer.

Go electric: Electric vehicles (EVs) cost more than petrol cars, but not for long: they're expected to reach 'price parity' starting from 2026 in some countries ... they're already cheaper in some countries that have incentivised take-up. Once bought, they're much cheaper to run as electricity is less expensive than petrol – especially if you can charge the car for free or from solar panels. The folks at My Electric Car estimate EVs are about 70% cheaper to run. The QLD government is a bit more conservative but they still say that if you drive 13,300 km a year, an electric car will cost about $1000 less to fuel.

FAQs

Why is petrol so expensive in Australia?

Tell that to a Kiwi and they'll laugh at you. Aussie petrol is cheap as, bro! They pay about 50c/L more than we do. Our fuel prices are high, but we're somewhere in the middle by international standards. The graph on the next page from the industry lobby group shows how good we have it.

I think we get all wound up about petrol prices because we're a nation of commuters and we drive a lot, and because they go up and down so much that we feel like someone somewhere overseas is having a lend of us.

Obviously we don't have oil reserves in Australia, so it has to come from overseas and that leaves us at the mercy of international wholesale prices and the value of the Aussie dollar.

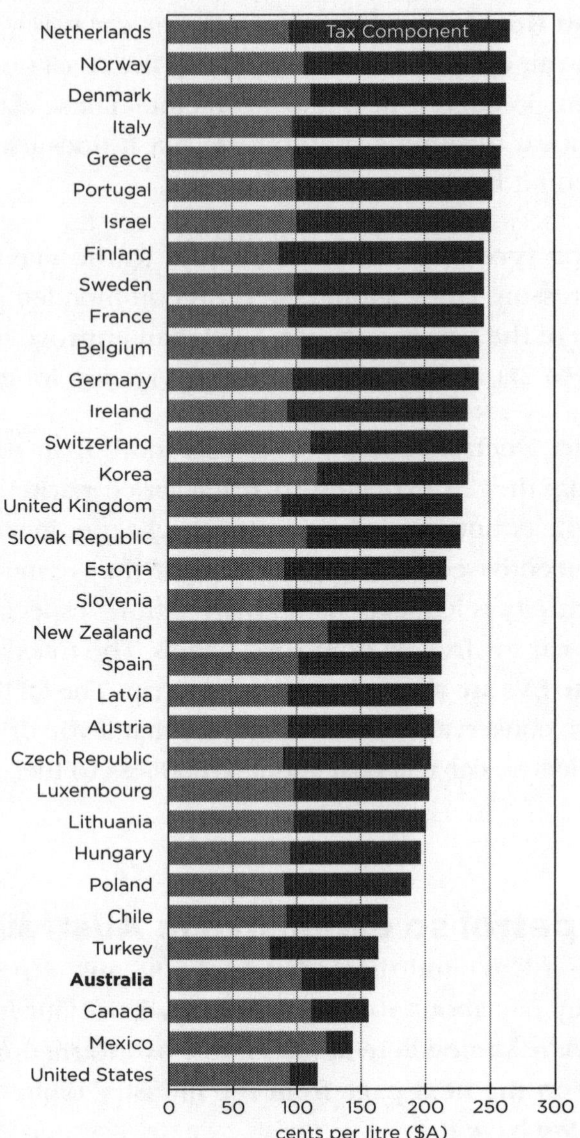

Source: Australian Petroleum Statistics, Office of the Chief Economist.

NUMBER CRUNCH

Average fuel prices have more than doubled since 2002 when they were around 87c/L, according to the Australian Institute of Petroleum.

Why do petrol prices fluctuate so much?

Pump prices at your local servo are influenced by the Singapore wholesale price of petrol (otherwise known as the Singapore Mogas 95 Unleaded Price, to your average petroleum industry geek), plus taxes and importing costs.

The Mogas 95 price is in turn influenced by international oil prices, which go up and down based on demand around the world and how much the oil-producing nations decide to produce (and they have a history of under-supplying the demand to protect their margins).

Below is a graph from the ACCC showing how our prices sort of follow the international benchmark price, but not always . . .

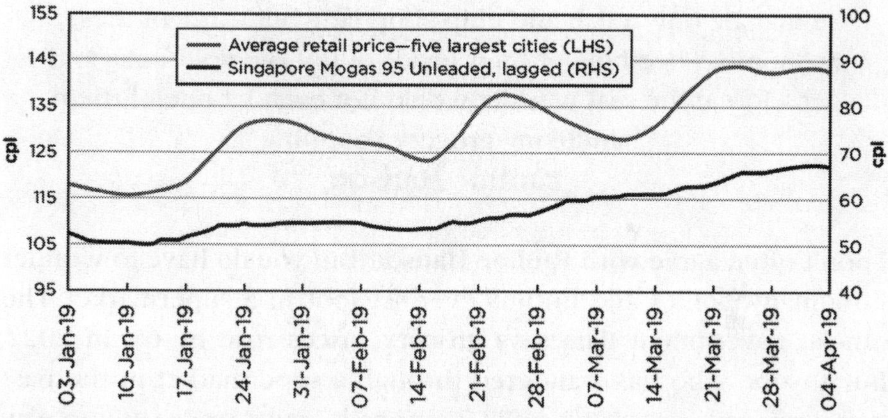

Source: ACCC © Commonwealth of Australia

Which state has the most expensive petrol?

Queenslanders, you're not imagining it! Brisbane usually has the priciest petrol out of the five major capitals, according to the ACCC. Perth occasionally topples Brisvegas from its pedestal, though, and Adelaide is the home of Australia's cheapest fuel on average.

Does petrol cost more in the bush?

It sure does, and not just in the bush proper. Anywhere outside metro Australia, the price goes up. In 2018, the annual average difference between regional prices and those in the five largest cities was 6.9c/L.

CHAPTER 21
GROCERIES

> 'I may be only a fish and chip shop lady, but some of these economists need to get their heads out of the textbooks and get a job in the real world. I would not even let one of them handle my grocery shopping.'
> **Pauline Hanson**

I don't often agree with Pauline Hanson, but you do have to wonder how many pollies and boffins ever set foot in a supermarket. The official government data says grocery prices rose by 6% in 2022. But anyone who has wandered through a supermarket in the past two years can see what's really happened – most prices are up way more than 6%. We've even seen $12 lettuces and steak that was priced more like lobster, after supply chain shemozzles and major floods on the east coast.

So just browsing the supermarket and tossing stuff in the trolley is no longer an option for money-savers: we've got to shop smart and beat the supermarkets at their own game.

If you can save $40 on the weekly shop, that's over $2000 a year, so every little saving counts. Let's find the easiest ones and go from there.

In a nutshell

Potential saving	Anywhere from $1000–$5000/year
Easiest	'Cheat on your supermarket'
Next-easiest	'Plan your raid' and 'Shop smart'
Top tools	Online catalogues and bulk-buys
If I could tell you one thing about grocery bills it would be:	Don't put all your eggs in one trolley!

CHEAT ON YOUR SUPERMARKET

Potential saving: Around $1600/year

Don't give all your love to one supermarket. Grocery shopping is not like a marriage or a football team – you don't have to be loyal. Here are three ways to cheat that can save you some easy money:

1. Go to Coles or Woolies if you need to, but try Aldi too. Aldi's the cheapest – there's no doubt about it. I've found my own weekly shop was about 10% less at Aldi, CHOICE research has found the difference on like-for-like baskets is 7–9% and Aldi's own research undertaken by PricewaterhouseCoopers says the difference depends on whether you compare them to name brands at the big supermarkets (around 25% more or $2468) or home brands (about 15% more or $1555).

For example, they sell a litre of olive oil for just $8–$10, and their premium dishwasher tablets are rated the best by CHOICE despite the fact they cost less than half what the name brands in Coles and Woolworths do.

In one experiment, I calculated that I can save around $1600 a year on my family's grocery bill if I stop in at Aldi too every week, compared to only shopping at Coles.

Even if you can't do it every week, shopping at two supermarkets now and then will save you money.

Insider Trick: The Mystery-Shopper

Usually this trick is about going undercover to see if a retailer is treating you right. But in this case, relax ... someone's already done the legwork for you.

In 2015, 2017 and 2021, consumer group CHOICE sent their undercover mystery shoppers into over 100 supermarkets in 30+ locations across Australia.

They priced a basket of 29–33 grocery items and then they compared the cost of the basket at each supermarket and averaged them out.

The finding? Aldi was cheaper, all three times.

There's not a great deal of difference between Coles and Woolworths pricing, probably because they monitor each other so closely.

Source: CHOICE

But if you're prepared to forgo the name brands at Coles and Woolies, CHOICE found you'd save an average of 53% with Aldi's budget products.

Even when you look at like-for-like comparisons, Aldi was on average 7.4% cheaper than Coles and Woolies for home brand products and 9% cheaper than Coles and Woolies for budget brand products.

Now, Aldi ain't for everyone. Some people swear by it; they love the dairy and the meat and the weird middle aisle that features everything from ski gear to onesies.

But others say they just can't get their heads around it; they love their big brands too much, or they hate packing their own groceries (one way Aldi keeps its prices down), or they just don't have an Aldi nearby.

At last count, the German raider had almost 600 stores across the country. In mid-2018, they became the most trusted brand in Australia, according to researcher Roy Morgan's Net Trust Score.

2. Go to a bulk-buy place from time to time: The occasional visit to a bulk-buy warehouse such as Costco or Campbells Wholesale (formerly known as 'Campbells Cash & Carry') allows you to buy non-perishables at cheap prices in large quantities and store them, saving hundreds in a year.

They usually have an annual membership fee (Costco's is $60, for example) but it won't take you long to make that back. Costco also has the cheapest petrol in town, for example, so fill up the car while you're there and you'll save around

$15 a tank, then buy 160 dishwasher tablets for around half the price per tablet they'll cost you at Coles. You could also go with a friend or family member and split the big-box items between you (and why not split the cost of the membership while you're at it!). Bulk-buying was one of the hacks recommended by mum of 11 Heather McIntyre when she was interviewed by the *Daily Telegraph* for her top grocery-saving tips. She uses a wholesaler called ABCOE in NSW.

3. Hit the farmers markets too sometimes. The fruit and vegetable markets are known to be cheaper, so if there's one near you then cash in. *The Daily Mail* bought a list of 19 fruits and vegetables at a market and a Woolworths on the same Friday in 2022 and found the markets were about half the price – $59.75 as opposed to $109.50. Produce at the markets can also be fresher and longer-lasting than supermarkets. Did you know that some supermarket apples have been in storage for almost a year?!

Insider Trick: The De Niro

The supermarkets' strategy is this: get you in the door with half-price specials or cheap milk or convenience, then use every trick in their books to 'increase your basket size' by enticing you to buy more while you're there – ideally your entire list, and ideally as many high-margin items in highly visible spots as possible.

But if you only buy the cheap stuff at one supermarket, then head next door to buy their cheap stuff too, you can beat them at their game and save thousands of dollars over time.

For most of us, this is our second biggest bill. You do your weekly shop and you only buy 50 or 100 different items that all cost not much, but they add up to an average of $240, according to the ABS's Household Expenditure Survey. That's $12,000 a year.

Big bills mean big potential savings, even if it's the sum of lots of little wins. Find a way to reduce the cost of every item by 20%, for example, and there's a potential saving on offer of over $2500 a year for that average household.

PLAN YOUR RAID

Potential saving: Around $1600/year

Make a list: It seems obvious, but saving on groceries starts with good planning, and good planning starts with a list. A list also makes you less prone to browsing, making impulse buys and throwing away stuff you didn't need. If I go shopping without a list I find I can fall into a state of 'grocery hypnosis' and come home with a trolley full of Tim Tams and pastrami. Not good.

Check out the weekly specials first: These become available on Wednesdays at all the major chains but they're advertised from 5pm Monday in their online catalogues. That means you can check them when making your list and raid the specials at more than one supermarket. There are two ways to check the specials: via a grocery savings app, or on the supermarket websites.

Insider Trick: David's Slingshot

A variety of apps can now scrape the supermarket catalogues each week and summarise the specials for you. I usually just browse the catalogues but take a look and see what works for you.

Frugl Grocery (on the App store or Google Play): Scans the full Coles and Woolies catalogues so you can search for any product and see which supermarket has it cheapest near you this week.

Half Price (on the App store or Google Play): Scans the catalogues for half-price specials to let you know what's 50% off, so you can stock up on things you need when they're cheap or plan your list around them.

Shopfully (on the App store or Google Play): Collects all the catalogues in one place so you can look at them before you hit the shops.

Coles
Download the 'Coles' app, subscribe to Flybuys, or check the website: www.coles.com.au/catalogues-and-specials/view-all- available-catalogues

Woolworths
Download the 'Woolworths' app, subscribe to Everyday Rewards, or check the website: www.woolworths.com.au/shop/catalogue

Aldi
Download the 'Aldi Australia' app, subscribe to the weekly email newsletter, or check the website catalogues for weekly 'Super Savers' specials: www.aldi.com.au/en/groceries/super-savers/

CONSUMER PSYCHOLOGY 101: Supermarket design

Supermarkets have a pricing strategy that uses certain specials as 'bait' to get you in the door and then certain other products as their margin-makers.

The cheap milk at the back of the shop? Probably one of the most successful baiting strategies ever invented, even if it has squeezed some dairy producers to near-bankruptcy …

The weekly specials? Also designed to get you in the door, even if they sometimes make a loss on those items.

On the other hand, the Tim Tams and fresh raspberries lovingly presented on the end of the aisle so you must walk past them to get to the cheap milk? That's often where they make their moolah, and it's also where your bill can blow out.

So you'll need to be aware of the tactics they use to make you spend more:

The layout: The shop is designed to maximise the time you spend there and 'cross-sell' you high-margin items that probably weren't on your list. IKEA is the worst example of this – it makes you follow a single, meandering path through every section if you want to get out of the place, but supermarkets do a bit of this too. The milk is up the back. The expensive health foods are often on the way from the entrance to the milk. The cheapest products are on the higher and lower shelves with the more expensive ones at eye level. Look up! Look down! Close your eyes as you walk past the Tim Tams.

The checkout: From magazines to chewie, chocolate and batteries, they use the checkout to suggest to you a final couple of small purchases while you wait in line. Ker-ching! They also use them to entice the kids to pester you to buy stuff that's no good for them. Resist!

Smells and sounds: The best exponents of this one are those Danish ice-cream shops that pump out the waffle-cone smell to entice you in. Gets me every time. But supermarkets do a bit of this too sometimes, pumping out the smell of baking bread and using music to make you comfortable and keep you wandering the aisles for longer. There's even research to show that playing French music makes people more likely to buy French food, and so on.

End-of-aisle displays: These are highly visible spots that they can sell to a particular brand or use to push a high-margin product. It's not the best place to buy your Tim Tams. If Tim Tams are on your list, at least go to the biscuit section where you can see what's on the high and low shelves, use the unit pricing and grab any specials that week.

The Aldi middle aisle: Aldi's famous twice-weekly 'Special Buys' each Wednesday and Saturday feature discount items in their middle aisle such as furniture and electrical goods. There's a theme each week (one week: ski gear, next week: garden tools) and most Aldi shoppers have a story about going out for some milk and coming home with a footbath! My tip for the middle aisle is to avoid browsing it – check the catalogue before you go and if you see a pair of lederhosen you absolutely must have (and this is a real example – my friend Chris Zinn bought exactly that), then zero in on said item when you arrive at the shops before moving onto the rest of your list. Remember: the middle aisle is the Bermuda Triangle of supermarket money-saving expeditions. Many a frugal shopper has walked by, glanced sideways at some 100% merino undergarments and never. Been. Seen. Again.

SHOP SMART

Potential saving: Around $600/year

There are a bunch of little things we can do when shopping that will add up to bigger savings over time, too. They're just what you might call good supermarket hygiene for us money-savers. None of them are difficult on their own, but some are time-consuming so we all just need to adopt the ones that we have the time and energy for, and don't sweat the rest. Up to you. Here are some ideas:

Declare a war on waste: Make a rough meal plan for the week, and try to use up what you have for starters. Play 'surprise chef' with the contents of the back of your cupboard. Each household wastes $1000 a year on average according to the NSW Government's 'Food Waste Avoidance Benchmark Study' in 2016.

Never shop when hungry: The hungrier you are, the more likely you are to … you guessed it: impulse buy. Approximately 57% of all Tim Tam purchases are made by hungry supermarket shoppers. (I made that statistic up – I don't actually know the figure for sure – but it is based on extensive first-hand research.)

Don't shop with kids (if possible) and NEVER shop with hungry kids: My kids once surprised me by saying they *liked* doing the shopping. 'Are you serious?' I asked. 'It means we get to beg for treats,' they said. So now I never take them to the supermarket if I can avoid it. I know that some of you never really have a choice, and you have my utmost sympathy. I always smile at the people with kids in the supermarket. They must wonder what I'm mugging at. But shopping with kids can be a cruel form of torture. It takes you longer, you get ground down by 'pester power', and you can't properly concentrate on money-saving strategies such as . . .

Use 'unit pricing': Consumer groups fought hard to make grocery retailers say on their price tags what the cost of almost every product is per 100 grams. So make the most of it. This way you can take two different products in different-sized packets (or two packets of the *same* product in different sizes) and see how the prices *really* compare.

Standard units: Most grocery items use a standard unit of measurement from the list below.

Type of item	Unit of measurement
Supplied by weight	per 100 grams
Supplied by volume	per 100 millilitres
Supplied by length	per metre
Supplied by area	per square metre
Supplied by number	per item included

Other units: Some grocery items use different units. For example, fruits and vegetables (per kilogram or per item), meat, seafood and poultry (per kilogram or per item) and drinks (per litre).

So look for the product that has the lowest unit price and opt for that – provided you're not buying such big portions that it'll go to waste, of course.

Ever tried shopping at night? There are a few reasons for the theory that it's cheaper to shop on, say, a Wednesday night than a Sunday morning. First, if you do it after dinner, you won't be hungry.

Second, there are often end-of-day specials and price reductions as supermarkets try to get rid of stock - especially baked goods, fresh produce and other perishables.

And third, crowds - or the lack of them. A more relaxed supermarket might be a better environment for a well-planned shop without impulse buys. Or so the theory goes. (Me? I'm usually too busy watching Netflix with a beer or vino after dinner. But each to their own.)

Buy the ugly fruit and veg: As I said above, we waste an average of $1000 per household per year and the #1 thing we throw out is fruit and veg. Most supermarkets now sell 'imperfect picks' or 'odd bunch' produce, which is all good on the inside even if it's no oil painting on the outside. And it's up to 50% cheaper.

Avoid packaging where you can: It costs money to put stuff in packets and that cost will end up factored into the price. As a general rule, you'll pay less for unpackaged items (although do check the unit pricing in any case).

Shop weekly, not daily: There's always going to be those mid-week trips to restock bread and milk and whatever, but if you do your big shop once a week for non-perishables and meat, you'll minimise the number of impulse buys.

Eyes up! Eyes down! Like a lot of other shops, supermarkets put the high-margin products at eye-level where you're most likely to see them. They even charge those manufacturers extra for eye-level shelving or end-of-aisle displays. Chances are, the stuff with the lowest unit pricing will be on the top shelves or the bottom shelves.

Don't shop online – unless you're an inveterate impulse buyer: Online shopping is hugely convenient. But if you want to maximise savings, it's not always ideal. There are a few reasons why: First, in the supermarket you can look up and down on the shelves and compare unit prices at a glance, whereas on the app or website that's much harder. Second, you'll often pay delivery charges. And third, bricks and mortar shops are often cheaper. As I said above, prices differ from shopping centre to shopping centre based on the level of competition. Online, you don't get the benefit of that. According to a 2016 mystery-shop by Fairfax Media, buying groceries online can attract a 10% premium on the same products.

The exception to this rule is that if you're an impulse-buyer, you might be less likely to do it when shopping online. So each to their own.

Insider Trick: The Red Dog

If you don't have the time (or frankly, you can't be bothered) shopping at more than one supermarket, fair enough.

But you can still be smart about your weekly Coles or Woolies shop.The Red Dog is a calculated tactic whereby you show kelpie-like levels of loyalty to a provider because they make it worth your while.

There are different reasons to pick and stick with each of the three biggest supermarket chains. Which one works for you will come down to your circumstances, really – which ones are nearby, where you buy your petrol, whether you prefer lowest prices or maximum rewards.

They also reward you for taking other products with them, such as telco plans, insurance or credit cards. For example, Woolworths rewards customers who take up its other products such as mobile plans and insurance policies by giving them 10% off one shop each month.That can be pretty generous if you do a big grocery shop of say $150 or $300 and stock up on pantry items and items that are on special.

The other way to access this discount is by joining their new 'Everyday Extra' rewards program for $59/year, which also includes 10% off a Big W shop each month. So if you normally spend around $600 or more at those two stores each year, it could be a no-brainer.

True Story: Leanne The Super-Switcher Aces Supermarket Rewards Schemes

Remember Leanne the super-switcher from Part 1? She got in touch again to share her tips on 'milking' supermarket rewards programs for maximum value. She's in the top 1% of Flybuys points collectors in Australia, even though she's shopping for just three people. She estimates she saved almost $1400, or 10% of her grocery bill, in a year by understanding how the algorithms work and chasing the best bonus point offers. (Almost 200,000 of her 220,000 Flybuys points were bonus points.)

Sophisticated rewards programs, such as Flybuys and Everyday Rewards, have software programs that monitor what we buy and what we click on, then send us tailored bonus-point offers to encourage us to buy more of the same thing.

However, canny shoppers can observe patterns in the algorithms and make the most of them. Here are some of her best strategies:

- 'Don't go over your limit in an offer. To do this I'll often do part of the shop on my partner's card and part on mine . . . the register staff don't mind you paying in two transactions – you just have to speak up and ask.'
- 'Play hard to get. If you stick to your limit, or you don't use the card for a couple of weeks, the algorithm often lowers the limit and makes a better offer.'

- 'Sometimes offers overlap. I had one recently that was 10,000 points for a $230 spend in one week and another offer of 8000 points for spending $220 a week for two weeks. So, I could get the 18,000 points as both offers were current.'
- 'If I don't have a good offer at Coles one week, I shop at Woolworths and delay any non-essentials until next week. This also encourages the algorithm to improve my offers.'
- 'Look at bonus products. They don't pay much usually, but there was a weird one at Christmas of 4000 points on a ham, so I timed when I bought my ham.'
- 'Don't redeem points in the online shop. You can find these products elsewhere and the best value for your points is to redeem them on grocery shopping.'
- 'Flybuys has added Bunnings and Officeworks, so we scan there too now.'

CHAPTER 22
HOME LOANS & RENT

> 'We're adding a little something to this month's sales contest. As you all know, first prize is a Cadillac El Dorado. Anyone wanna see second prize? Second prize is a set of steak knives. Third prize is you're fired.'
>
> **Alec Baldwin as a real estate agent in *Glengarry Glen Ross***

It's a brutal time to be the proud owner of a mortgage in Australia – let alone a first-home buyer.

In 2022, our good friends on the Reserve Bank board gave the average home borrower a $9,000 price hike. That's how much the cost of interest on the average $620,000 mortgage increased in just over half a year, after they'd promised not to lift rates until 2024.

So while power prices and insurance premiums and petrol and grocery bills all played their part in creating the biggest cost of living crisis in a generation, it's home loans that really blew the top off.

Even if you're a renter, chances are your landlord's increased mortgage costs are now being passed onto you, at least in part.

Saving thousands on a mortgage is not always easy because there's a lot of red tape involved and they're complicated financial products. But there is plenty we can do to try, and by now you're well and truly ready.

If you've read this book from the beginning, you're now the Ralph Macchio of money-saving and this is like the final fight in

The Karate Kid where you whip out the crane kick and finish off your floppy blond-haired nemesis.

This bill is the biggest of them all. But the bigger they are, the harder they fall. Shave even 0.50% off here and it could save you tens of thousands of dollars over time.

So let's see if we can put some cash back in your pocket.

In a nutshell

Potential saving	Thousands of dollars a year
Easiest	'Just ask' and 'Switch'
Next-easiest	'Tweak your loan' and 'Government leg-ups'
Top tools	Brokers and Joust.com.au
If I could tell you one thing about mortgages it would be:	Even a small rate cut could save you as much as your power bill!

JUST ASK

Potential saving: $2000 a year

Go on. Call your lender and ask for a rate discount. What's the worst thing that could happen? People never think this will work, but in my experience it gets a result about half of the time.

Ideally, get yourself some leverage first. Check a comparison site such as Canstar.com.au, RateCity.com.au or Finder.com.au and make a note of what the lowest advertised rates are right now.

NUMBER CRUNCH

It costs a mortgage provider more than $1000 and often over $1500 in advertising and other costs for each new customer they attract. So if they're thinking straight, they should be prepared to give you hundreds in savings to stop you leaving.

If you have over 20% equity in your home, and your mortgage is for a large amount, that makes you the Chris Hemsworth or Margot Robbie of mortgage customers – you are very attractive! So be sure to tell them that too.

Use this script as a starting point or, if you have a broker, ask them to make the call for you:

> *'Hi, my name is* [Insert Your Name Here] *and I've been a customer for ______ years. I've just noticed my interest rate is ______% p.a. and there are now rates out there of ______% p.a. with _____ and _____% p.a. with _____. So I'm planning on switching – especially given I own over 20% of my home and I'm borrowing a large amount so I'm confident I'll be able to get an extra rate discount. But I just thought I'd make one call to see if you can match it before I request a mortgage discharge form. What's the best rate you can offer me to stay?'*

SWITCH!

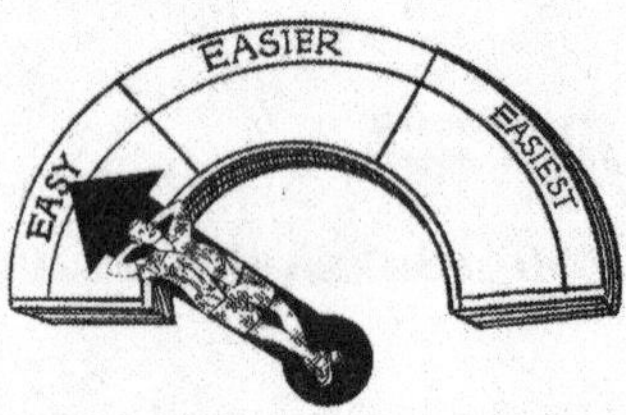

Potential saving: $2000 a year

If the bank won't play ball and you feel like you have other options, call their bluff.

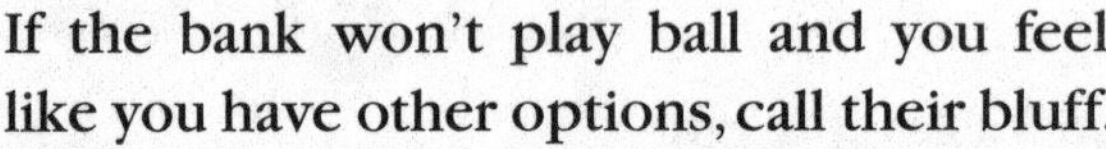

The De Niro savings trick outlined in Part 2 can save you more money on this bill than any other. As in most industries, it's the borrowers who are *prepared to switch* who get the best results – even if you end up staying put.

NUMBER CRUNCH

The Reserve Bank says the average gap between 'new customer' rates and 'old customer' rates is 0.47%.

But comparison site RateCity.com.au looked at the Big Four Banks in mid-2022 and found that there was an enormous difference ranging from 0.90% to 1.39%.

On a $500,000 loan, that's a difference of between $3000 and $4656 in the first year!

Switching rates in banking are far too low. Governments for years have talked a good game about fixing this but at the end of the day, Australians have decided it's still a hassle. We're more likely to get divorced than to break up with our bank, and about 40% of us are still with the first bank we ever opened an account with.

The banks know this and they 'bank' on you staying put. But if you're prepared to move, then you can take the upper hand – because this is one industry where there are more than fifty different options to choose from!

True Stories: There Are De Niros Giving Their Banks Hell All Over The Place, Just Ask Around

I did a little experiment. I whacked the following question up on Facebook just to see how many De Niros there were out there playing hardball with their lenders.

'Anyone had success negotiating their mortgage lender down to a lower rate – or switching to another lender – recently? I'm writing something about home loans and keen to hear people's experiences.'

I might as well have asked who makes the best coffee in Melbourne. I was inundated.

My buddy Joanne: 'Yep. Two or three times. CBA. We just ring and ask for an extra discount every now and then and they reluctantly agree. Weird.'

My old workmate Nick: 'Commonwealth ignored my query, so we went to a smaller bank, IMB, that massively undercut them and did all the legwork for me. Current rate is 3.59%. Earlier one was well over 4%. Let's have a red wine lunch later in winter!'

My old high school pal Dave: 'Hey, mate. So every year we review. We originally got our loan through a broker. It is with Citibank and is a full service loan. Last year, we got an offer from a new broker for a much better rate. I called Citi and within 20 minutes they dropped the rate from 3.93% to 3.69%. They moved rates up in January to 3.85% and last month HSBC approached us with a rate of 3.75%. So I called Citi again and they dropped the rate again to 3.79%. We will now check every six months!'

My brother's mate Jared: 'I had two mortgages with Westpac for over 12 years and moved to HSBC for a new purchase . . . Westpac failed to match so I subsequently moved my other mortgage products to HSBC out of principle.'

My friend Amber: 'We have our home loan with NAB. [My husband's] business does their banking with CBA and they approached him with an offer if we moved our home loan to them – they would reduce our interest rate and have zero fees. We took that to NAB and basically said 'match this or we walk' and they matched it.'

And this – equally inspirational if not very helpful – from my dad: 'Getting rid of a mortgage is a great feeling.'

Insider Trick: David's Slingshot

Unlike insurance, where you can't really compare prices online, home loan options are very easy to navigate on the internet.

This bill gets more complicated once you start applying for loans and you have to deal with qualification processes and paperwork, but the first bit – taking a look at what's out there – is easy. You've got a few options:

Slingshot #1 – Comparison websites

Just go to one of the bigger comparison sites such as RateCity.com.au, Canstar.com.au or Finder.com.au, punch in your details, and see what they kick out.

You'll need to decide what 'features' you can't do without. Need an offset account? Some cheap loans don't have them. A redraw facility? Ditto. Not prepared to leave the big banks? Be prepared to pay a bit more for the privilege. Once you know your non-negotiables, you can adjust your search accordingly.

Remember to look at the 'Comparison Rates'. These are a godsend from regulators because they adjust the advertised interest rate to include any other fees that apply on the loan in the first year.

These sites really are very easy to use, and they often have special offers on them too that are even better than the standard deal.

PRO TIP

Most sites will show you 'promoted' or 'partner' offers first. Look for a link or a button that says 'show all offers' or 'show offers without links' to get the whole picture.

Slingshot #2 – 'Robo-brokers'

If you don't want to hunt around on a comparison site for interest rates, and you don't have a good broker to do it for you, there's a range of new tools you can try out. Let's call them 'Robo-brokers'.

Technology catches up with all of us eventually, and now it's evolving in the mortgage business too, as web developers race to replace human brokers with these 'online home loan marketplaces' that collect your data and then shop *you* around to brokers and lenders.

One of the advantages of these platforms is that – like a real broker – once they know a bit about you they can hunt down loans that you're likely to be approved for. Chances are you won't know this yourself when browsing the cheapest loans on comparison websites above, and many of those cheapest loans are only available to the most desirable borrowers.

So if you're serious about finding a low rate and you don't want to do your own searching, by all means give one of these guys a go. I made inquiries with the ones below for research purposes and within minutes I had several offers to compare – including both big and small banks. Once you get an offer from them, the power is in your hands: you can either take it up or see if your current lender will match it.

Joust.com.au

A 'live auction' site where you answer a short list of questions about yourself and 'up to 80% of home loan lenders' then bid for your business.

They check your credit score but it's not affected by this 'soft inquiry'.

I received multiple offers within twenty-four hours - many via brokers so this is also a way to connect with a new broker.

Lendi.com.au

A mortgage marketplace where you answer a longer list of questions about yourself - essentially you fill out an online mortgage application form - and you then receive offers from brokers.

So you'll need all your info handy, but you can do it entirely online if you want to.

BROKER? OR NO BROKER?

This is a big question you'll need to answer for yourself and the answer can change over time.

Imagine every time you went to a petrol station to fill up, they asked you your bank balance, your employment status and your spending habits, and then charged you a price based on how financially secure you are.

Because that's how the mortgage industry works. It's like shopping in Bali: everyone pays a different price, only a mug pays the advertised rate, and no matter how well you do, you always wonder if someone else is paying less.

Banks advertise their 'standard variable rate' (SVR) but behind the scenes, how much you pay all comes down to how well you haggle and what sort of a customer you are.

And that's the main reason why about half of all home loans in this country are sorted by a broker, I reckon. Aussies love Bali, but we hate to haggle! And we're more than happy to let someone else do it for us (especially if someone else is paying them and we can't get a much better result doing it ourselves).

I use a broker, but it's not always necessary. I think it depends on what sort of person you are, and what your current circumstances are.

Confident haggler? Internet savvy? Full-time job? Simple application? Like your smaller, challenger brands and keen to kiss the Big Four goodbye? Well then, it sounds like you're the 'no broker' type to me, especially if you have the time to research online and deal direct with your lender.

Hate haggling? Not computer-savvy? Self-employed or a complicated application? Or super-busy with a young family and no time for admin? Maybe a broker's for you. Here are some of the pros and cons of using a broker:

PROs:

- **Discounts:** Brokers can sometimes get a better deal than you from certain lenders because they buy 'wholesale'. The flipside of this is that they often steer you towards the lenders they prefer to deal with (or who pay them more). So they may not compare the whole market for you. (In fact, they almost certainly won't compare lenders who don't pay brokers!)
- **Paperwork:** Brokers take care of a lot of the red tape involved in a loan application, which can be mind-numbingly boring and time-consuming for those of us who don't deal with it day-in, day-out.
- **Customer service:** Brokers are middlemen and middlewomen. They save you time comparing loans and when dealing with banks and other lenders, it can be a relief to have someone in your corner to stick up for you or push their weight around if need be.
- **Knowledge:** A good broker knows which banks are the best to deal with in certain circumstances. I'm a sole trader, for example, and some of them won't lend to me.

CONs:

- **Control:** Brokers' commissions get bigger according to how much business they can send to a particular lender. So using a broker might mean you're channelled towards a particular product, when you wanted someone to compare the whole market for you.
- **Risk:** Brokers' clients tend to borrow more and take on more risky loans such as interest-only loans, according to research by ASIC. This may be because brokers are paid according to the size of the loan so it's in their interest for you to borrow more.
- **Cost:** Brokers get over $2 billion in commissions a year and that adds 16 basis points to the cost of the average home loan, according to a UBS report. (On the other hand, in most cases you pay that extra amount whether you use a broker or not, so you might as well get the free service . . .)
- **Range:** You can't get some of the cheapest loans through a broker. HSBC, a big international bank that offers some of the lowest rates around, doesn't deal with most brokers. Ditto a lot of the lenders with the cheapest rates advertised online – they're cheaper because they don't factor in the average $3000 that others pay a broker for a loan!

Brokers are supposed to be upfront with you about how they get paid. So get on the front foot and ask them some questions like these at your first meeting – or maybe even 'interview' them by email before you decide who to meet:

1. How many lenders do you deal with?
2. Which lender do you put the most loans through and why?
3. What are the upfront costs of the loan?
4. Are you a member of the MFAA? (The peak body for mortgage brokers in Australia, which requires members to abide by a Code of Practice.)
5. I just found an interest rate of [insert low rate] at the comparison website [insert website name]. Can you beat that?

A broker could also give you advice on when is the right time to-refinance. The pros include accessing a lower rate; accessing equity in your home to renovate, invest or buy something; and maybe paying off the loan faster. Or your life might have changed and you might just need a feature you didn't need before, such as an offset account or a redraw facility or a line-of-credit home loan.

On the other hand, it costs money to close out one loan and open another, and the timing might not be ideal if your home value has just dropped, so check the costs and factor that in. The fees can include:

- discharge fee, to get out of your old loan: \$200–\$400;
- exit fee (if you took our your loan before July 2011, or you have a fixed rate loan): can cost thousands;
- application/establishment fees for the new loan: \$200–\$600;
- valuation fees, to pay an independent valuer to assess the property: \$300;
- settlement fees, for the lender to arrange the funding: \$100–\$300;
- legal fees, for the lender's solicitor: \$75–\$150;
- package fees, a monthly cost that some lenders charge in exchange for giving you a discount on the variable rate: \$100–\$500; and/or
- lender's mortgage insurance, if you're borrowing over 80% of the property value: can cost thousands.

True Story: My Mortgage Broker Feeds My Dog Chicken Breast

We met our broker because a real estate agent told us he'd arranged her loan. *Why would a real estate agent need a broker?* I thought. But over time it's become obvious how brokers can earn their keep, no matter how savvy you are about property.

First, he switched us from one bank to another. We weren't too fussed about which lender we were with as long as the rate was low. He has purchasing power with a particular bank because he puts a lot of business through them and he's part of a network of brokers who do the same.

To some extent, interest rates are set in stone: if you borrow $X and you have $Y of equity in your home, you'll get a 1% or a 1.5% discount on the standard variable rate.

But there's a tiny bit of wriggle room: when there are line-ball calls, your broker can make an application to the bank's 'pricing department' for a slightly better deal, and sometimes you'll get it.

When I became self-employed, he knew which banks would probably lend to us and which ones wouldn't.

These days, our broker makes donations to our kids' school fundraisers and feeds my dog chicken breast.

He's sorted out several administrative shemozzles for us over the years and he's haggled them down to a lower rate on about three occasions.

He's getting paid by the bank to keep us happy and that's fine with me (and with Sunny, my dog). If the day comes when he can't help us out anymore, then we'll switch!

TWEAK YOUR LOAN

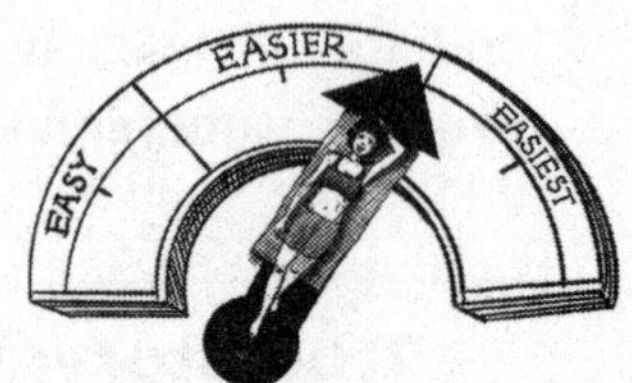

Potential saving: $1000 a year

There are a range of tweaks you can make to your home loan to put some money back into your pocket. If you're a 'mortgage prisoner', who can't switch, these might be the only options available to you. Mortgage prisoners are people who took out their loan when rates were lower and home values were higher, and can't re-finance because their borrowing capacity and/or home value has dropped.

Use an offset account: Not all loans feature this but many do. All it means is that you have an account (say, your savings or main transaction account) where the balance counts towards your mortgage, as if you've already paid it onto the mortgage. Therefore it reduces the amount you pay interest on while still giving you access to the money if you need it.

Use a redraw facility: This is very similar to an offset account, except it works the other way. You can take back money you've paid onto the mortgage, if you need it. An offset is considered better, simply because the money is still yours – banks can in theory refuse a request to redraw money.

Pay more than you have to: It's surprising how much an extra $100 a week or so can make your mortgage disappear more quickly. If you can afford to pay more than the minimum principal and interest payment your bank requires, do it. Make sure you're allowed to first (some fixed rate loans forbid it, for example). ASIC Moneysmart gives the following example:

Case Study: Jie and Ming save $65,000 and four years by paying extra

Let's say a young couple borrows $380,000 over twenty-five years at 6% p.a. (Not a good rate, but it's just a hypothetical example created by the financial watchdog's Moneysmart website . . .)

'Jie and Ming then realised that by making slightly higher repayments fortnightly (calculated by dividing the monthly payment by two), they would end up making an extra monthly payment each year. This would mean they could pay off the loan four years early and save about $65,000 in interest.'

Google 'ASIC mortgage calculator' to see how much you could shave off your loan by paying extra: www.moneysmart.gov.au/tools-and-resources/calculators-and-apps/mortgage-calculator#!how-can-i-repay-my-loan-sooner

Go interest-only (short-term solution only!): This will end up costing you more over the long run but if you've hit a rough patch where your income has dropped, one option is to move to an interest-only loan for a period of time. These became very popular from about 2010 to 2015 before regulators cracked down on them, so it's now harder to get approved and the rates are not as low as principal and interest loans. But because you're paying interest only, the repayments could be lower on these loans. Ask your broker or your bank first. A similar trick is to extend your loan over a longer period, which will also cost you more over time but reduce repayments in the short term.

Move or rent out a room: Renting out a property might mean you do not have to sell it. You might be able to 'negatively gear' your home while you live elsewhere as a 'rent-vester'. However, in this scenario, you still might have to pay land tax, a more expensive investment loan, and capital gains tax, if you eventually sell. It always pays to have a professional financial adviser crunch the numbers for you. The 'nuclear option' is to move out and sell.

Ask your bank for relief: If you're in financial trouble, every lender is required to have a 'hardship program' for people like you. Make sure you talk to them if you've missed a repayment or you're likely to, so they know why – and what they can do to help you get back on track. Mortgage repayment holidays no longer automatically damage your credit score. Lenders must record 'on-time payments' in each of the months they are paused. Instead, it is just noted on your credit record that you have a hardship agreement.

ASIC Moneysmart says these are the steps you need to apply for a 'hardship variation':

1. Contact your lender or credit provider – by phone or in writing.
2. Ask to speak to a 'hardship officer' or to customer service.

3. Give the details of your loan (account name and number, and the amount you pay each week/fortnight/month).
4. Say that you want to change your loan repayments because you are experiencing hardship (as set out in section 72 of the National Consumer Credit Code).
5. Explain why you are having difficulties making payments, how long you think your financial problems will continue and how much you can afford to repay.

The Financial Rights Legal Centre also creates sample letters you can use as a template at this address: financialrights.org.au/sample-letters/

If you are not satisfied with the lender's response you can contact the Australian Financial Complaints Authority (afca.org.au) on 1800 931 678. This is a free external dispute resolution scheme.

GOVERNMENT LEG-UPS

Potential saving: Up to $15,000

Most of these are targeted at first home-buyers. It's never been harder to buy your first home in Australia but I would argue there's also never been a broader range of help available as there is now, so if you're looking to buy, make sure you cash in. Some people will be able to access all of the below.

First Home Owner Grants: Eligibility varies from state to state and the rules change regularly so check them at FirstHome.gov.au. At the time of writing they were:

In NSW: $10,000 for the purchase or building of new homes valued at $750,000 or less, plus a waiver of stamp duty for homes (new or otherwise) under $800,000.

In QLD: $15,000 for the purchase or building of new homes valued at less than $750,000.

In VIC: $10,000 for the purchase or building of new homes (or $20,000 in regional Victoria) valued at $750,000 or less, plus a waiver of some or all stamp duty for homes (new or otherwise, and also available to pensioners and farmers).

In SA: $15,000 for the purchase or building of new homes valued at up to $575,000.

In WA: $10,000 for the purchase or building of new homes valued at up to $750,000 or $1 million (depending on where the home is).

In the ACT: Stamp duty concessions up to about $35,000 for all homes, means-tested.

In the NT: $10,000 for the purchase or build of new homes.

First Home Guarantee Scheme: This means you can buy with a 5% deposit. Usually you need to save 20% of the purchase price as a deposit, because if you have to borrow more than 80% of the price, you'll need lender's mortgage insurance (LMI), which adds another cost (and some lenders might even charge you a higher interest rate). But if you're one of 35,000 people each year to qualify for the First Home Guarantee Scheme, you'll be able to purchase with only a 5% deposit and the National Housing Finance and Investment Corporation will go guarantor for the remaining 15% so that you can avoid Lender's Mortgage Insurance.There are caps on how expensive the property can be, which are updated each year. In 2022, they ranged from $400,000 to $800,000 depending on where you bought. You must also be an owner-occupier who earnt no more than $125,000 last year or $200,000 as a couple.

Not everyone is a fan of buying with a low deposit, however. ASIC's Moneysmart, the Captain Sensible of money websites, says: 'The bigger your deposit, the less you have to borrow, and the more you will save in interest.'

Remember to factor in all the other nasty little surprises like stamp duty, legal fees, rates, home insurance and bank fees.

First Home Super Saver Scheme (FHSS): Can be used by first home buyers to save money towards a deposit at a lower tax rate inside their super fund. Couples, siblings, or friends can each access their own eligible FHSS contributions to purchase the same property. If any of you have previously owned a home, it will not stop anyone else who is eligible from applying. Talk to your super fund first. You can save:

- up to a maximum of $15,000 in any one financial year; and
- up to a maximum of $50,000 across all years.

Shared equity scheme: The federal government will co-own property with some first home buyers to help them get into the market for less. The Albanese government promised a new scheme with 10,000 places a year for first home buyers who earn $90,000 or less for individuals, or $120,000 or less for couples. 'Eligible home buyers will need a minimum deposit of 2%, with an equity contribution from the Federal Government of up to a maximum of 40% of the purchase price of a new home and up to a maximum of 30% of the purchase price for an existing home.' There are caps on the value of property you can buy under the scheme – they differ by state and city/region. Similar schemes are already operating in several states including WA and Victoria.

CHAPTER 23
LIFE INSURANCE

'There are only two stories in personal finance – "How much can you save?" and "Are you being ripped off?"'
Old newsroom saying

Bear with me here. The mere mention of Life Insurance can send some people into a hypnotic trance – not only is it boring but it involves thinking about death. But this bill is like the annual prostate check or pap smear that we're told to have as we get older: It's not most people's idea of fun, but it is good for you and the people you love!

So . . . this won't hurt a bit, and it will only take a minute or two. It's important you read this chapter because chances are you don't have enough life insurance and you could be paying too much for whatever you do have. Let's identify the easiest ways to do a quick, um, probe.

NUMBER CRUNCH

There were almost as many life insurance policies in Australia as people in 2019, thanks to our compulsory superannuation system. Most super funds have automatic insurance included – except for accounts with small balances and those owned by younger people because of some recent changes.

But how many of us know if we're getting good value for our money?

To make up for the subject matter, this will be the funniest chapter in this book. I've hidden six of the world's best dad jokes in it.

It will also be the only chapter where I suggest many of us should be spending MORE on a bill. You'll see why.

Skip these pages and you might not only go to your grave under-insured, but also dangerously under-amused.

In a nutshell

Potential saving	Up to $500/year
Easiest	'Super funds'
Next-easiest	'Direct life insurance'
Top tools	ASIC Moneysmart
If I could tell you one thing about life insurance it would be:	It's like spinach: it tastes like you-know-what but it's good for you

SUPER FUNDS

Potential saving: Around $500/year

An Irishman walks into a chemist and asks for some deodorant. 'The ball or the aerosol?' asks the chemist. 'No, the armpit,' says the Irishman. While you think about that one, here's how to quickly check if you have enough life insurance and how to use your super fund to top it up.

1. **First, work out how much cover you really need.** Do *not* use calculators on life insurers' websites, which have a curious tendency to over-inflate the number ... Use the ASIC Moneysmart life insurance calculator at this link: www.moneysmart.gov.au/tools-and-resources/calculators-and-apps/life-insurance-calculator
2. **Second, check how much cover you have right now (in your super, and/or elsewhere).** For many of us, this number

will be smaller than the amount of cover we need, which means we're under-insured. Of course, if you have a partner with an income they should also have some life insurance, so you'll need to combine the amounts to see if you have enough.

3. **Ask your super fund how much it would cost to increase your cover to the amount you need.** This is the first port of call because super funds 'bulk-buy' life insurance and get a discount for doing so. This is called 'Group Life' in the industry. If your current life insurance was purchased through a financial adviser or planner, there's more likely to be a saving by getting a quote from your super fund.

INSIDE INFO

Actuaries are people who spend their days calculating the chances of things going wrong so that businesses can plan ahead – they're a bit like gamblers who bet on the losing horse instead of the winner.

Actuaries are not the life of the party. But they do have an irritating habit of being right, and they say that when it comes to life insurance, Australians are woefully underinsured.

According to Rice Warner, some of Australia's best-known actuarial experts on life insurance, Australians are under-insured and it's getting worse. They say:

'The median default cover of superannuation funds meets approximately 65% to 70% of basic level death cover needs for average households, but a much lower proportion for families with children.'

If you die at 60, Rice Warner reckons your family would need 1.6 years of family income to meet their basic needs if that happened (heaven forbid).

But die at 50, and they'll need 3.2 years of income, and kick the bucket at age 40 and they'll need 5.4 years of income just to get by.

Meanwhile, 30-year-old parents with kids, they say, should have:

- 8 times family income for life insurance;
- 4 times family income for TPD (total and permanent disability) insurance; and
- 85% of family income for income protection insurance.

That might sound like a lot of cover for a 30-year-old, but keep in mind these policies are cheaper when you're young. (A 30-year-old can get $500,000 of fully underwritten life cover for under $300 p.a. for a man and under $200 p.a. for a woman.)

Anyway, you get the idea. If most of us died or were too sick to work, our families would be up the creek with a paddle-pop stick. (By the way, what do you call a zoo with just one dog in it? A shih tzu.)

True Story: Adam Cut His Premiums By 10–12%

'I think my life insurance was a set and forget one. For at least 15–20 years I didn't really look at it.

'But I'm now saving between 10 and 12% on my annual premiums, and I can tell you that makes me feel pretty happy.

'Switching life insurance takes a little bit of time because there's a lot of questions and answers to go through . . . what you need in your cover and any pre-existing conditions you may have.

But other than that it was really easy. The company did all the prep work, sent through the documents, you check it and sign it and away you go.

'I say have a look at what you're paying. Don't just set and forget. Insurance companies love this, they just want you to roll over – but that's the worst thing you can do. You have to go back and you have to test the market. It's your money, you work hard for it, don't waste it.'

DIRECT LIFE INSURANCE

Potential saving: Around $500/year

EASY EASIER EASIEST

This is the other way to save on your premium, and it can sometimes be as easy as saving via group insurance in your super fund.

There are three broad types of life insurance and some are traditionally more expensive than others. Let's call them 'advised' life insurance, 'direct' life insurance and 'super' life insurance.

You can either buy life insurance through an adviser, or direct from an insurance company, or through your super fund. That's the main difference – where you buy them.

But direct life insurance and super fund life insurance tend to cost less.

That's because, until recently, financial advisers who sold you a life insurance policy were sometimes getting paid a finder's fee equal to your entire first year's premium by the life insurer! You don't need to be an actuary to see how that would have inflated premiums.

This cosy little rort has been cut back in recent years, with a new 'shrinking' cap on commissions of 60%. But if you want to see if you can save on life insurance, don't just get a quote through an adviser/broker/planner.

To be fair to advisers and brokers, ASIC data says that 'direct' life insurance has more claims rejected and more disputes, as this table shows: probably because life insurance via a broker or adviser is 'underwritten', meaning they ask you a bunch of questions and give you a price based on your personal circumstances, and your family then has someone to help them if they need to make a claim.

	Disputes per 100,000 lives insured	Claims accepted rate	Average claim time (months)
'Super' Life Insurance	1.4	98.3%	1.0
'Direct' Life Insurance	19.0	89.7%	2.8
'Advised' Life Insurance	7.4	97.1%	1.5

Source: ASIC Moneysmart

Some direct life insurance is also 'fully underwritten'.

Filling out an 'under-writing' form can be a boring half-hour at the time, but it can also mean that as long as you answer their questions truthfully, your claims are more likely to be paid (see the table above).

A fully under-written insurance contract also ensures that you can renew each year, regardless of any change in your medical condition, without the need for further underwriting.

Most advised life insurance works like this, but a handful of direct life insurers do it too.

Most direct life insurance, however, is not underwritten. It's 'one size fits all', and the downside of that seems to be that claims are rejected more often.

So get a quote from a direct life insurer who offers fully-underwritten cover if you want to minimise your costs and maximise the chances of the policy being paid out.

Insider Trick: The De Niro

If you've done everything in this book up to this point, you've got some serious money-saving chops by now and you know exactly what this trick is all about – flagrant disloyalty!

When it comes to blind loyalty and bills, life insurance might just be the worst of the bunch.

I say that because most life insurance policies are picked for us by a super fund, an adviser or a planner, which makes us less likely to know if we're getting good bang for our buck.

In fact, I'll be a monkey's uncle if most people can even name their life insurance company off the top of their head. (Speaking of animals, what do you call a cow with no legs? Ground beef.)

But life insurance is also one of the best bills to consider when you want to go hunting for a big saving, because of the fat that's built into a lot of premiums and because the premiums can get very steep in later life.

The financial advice and planning industries will not like this book, because it encourages people to wade into the quicksand of financial products and try to make their own way out.

Fair enough. If you've got a broker or adviser or planner, you *should* take their advice on which life insurance policy is the right one. They ought to know their stuff.

But you should also know that in most cases they're paid for referring you to a policy, and you can sometimes save a packet by cutting out the middleman.

Why not get an alternative quote yourself and show it to your adviser/planner/broker and see if they can beat it. That way you know that you're getting the best result – whether that's through them or 'DIY'.

You can then compare the alternative quote to what you're paying now, and if you're not getting good value for money, you can switch or put your current provider on the spot.

Here's a basic script for what you'll need to say:

> *'Hi, my name is* [Insert Your Name Here] *and I've been a customer for ______ years. I've just noticed I pay $______ for $______ of life insurance cover and there are other providers out there offering $______ of cover for $______, such as __________. So I'm planning on switching. But I just thought I'd make one final call to see if you can give me a better deal than the one I'm on. What's the best deal you can offer me to stay?'*

True Story: Entrepreneur Joanne Saves $1000 p.a. On Two Life Covers

This is Joanne Kennard from Brisbane. She's a keen camper and an ideas person. Her inventions include the 'Easy Oven', a slow cooker made of fabric, and the 'Bush Barbie', a highly-efficient wood camp stove.

All-up, she runs about five different start-ups and small businesses from home. So she knows a bit about managing budgets. But even Joanne was surprised at how much the price of life insurance can differ from one provider to the next.

'Years of loyalty doesn't mean anything,' she told me.

With their old life insurer, Joanne and her husband's life cover cost them $5823.72 per annum.

When they shopped around and got a quote from a direct life insurer offering fully underwritten cover, they were quoted $4464.24 per annum.

That's almost $1400 less. And they also got 'two months free' for joining, which means they saved over $2000 in the first year. #BillKilled!

Insider Trick: The Good Listener

Let's say you want to get a quote from a 'direct' life insurer to compare to the policy your super fund or your financial adviser has sold you.

How do you sort the good from the bad? It's an important question because direct life insurance policies are not all equal – some are pretty basic.

Fortunately, there are now a range of annual awards and star ratings for direct life insurance products that you can use to help sift the crap from the cream of the crop.

Financial comparison website Canstar has one of the best-known systems for rating these products.

Their experts assess each policy for 20 different types of customer across all ages, genders and smoker/non-smoker status. Then they apply a star rating for value based on its price competitiveness first (this makes up 70% of the rating), and features second (30% of the rating).

Their five-star products 'are the top 10% of products in their field', according to Canstar.

If it gets four stars, it has 'a good mix of price and features and shouldn't be struck off your shopping list, especially if the product and brand really appeal to you'.

You can check the latest results at their website but in 2022 the winners for direct life insurance were:

- NobleOak;
- RAA; and
- TAL.

(Full disclosure: I have a NobleOak policy because I like the fact that they offer fully-underwritten direct life cover, and we work with them to create special deals for our members at One Big Switch. What happened to the refrigerator saleswoman? Kelvinator.)

FAQs:

What's the difference between life, TPD, trauma and income protection insurance?

All these variations can sometimes be grouped under the general term 'life insurance' or 'risk insurance', but they're all slightly different:

- **Life cover,** a.k.a. 'term life insurance', a.k.a. 'death cover', pays a set amount of money when you die to the beneficiaries on your policy.
- **Total and permanent disability (TPD) cover** is often sold with life cover. It pays a lump sum if you are totally and permanently disabled. Note that some policies only cover you if you cannot undertake any occupation. The better ones cover you if you can't do your *own* occupation.
- **Trauma cover** pays out if you are diagnosed with certain illnesses such as cancer or a stroke.
- **Income protection cover** pays out if you can't work for a while because of injury or illness.
- **Accidental death cover** pays a set benefit if you die because of certain types of accident (as opposed to an illness or disease).

What's the difference between 'stepped premiums' and 'level premiums'?

Just like it says: one type goes up over time, the other stays flat. Stepped premiums go up as you get older because the actuaries believe you're more likely to make a claim. The annual step-ups in premiums are relatively modest for those aged under 40 but increase substantially as we get older; up to 10% or more per annum for those aged over 60. Most cover offered by Australian life insurers features stepped premiums.

Level premiums are usually quite high at younger ages but they don't feature the big increases as you get older. How many Spaniards does it take to change a lightbulb? Juan.

Does my insurer pay out?

Government regulator to the rescue! ASIC Moneysmart has a claims calculator that shows the record of various insurers when it comes to paying claims:

www.moneysmart.gov.au/tools-and-resources/calculators-and-apps/life-insurance-claims-comparison-tool

You made it. You're a money-saving ninja.

If you're reading this, and you didn't skip to this page, that means you've earnt your money-saving Black Belt.

Hopefully you've put hundreds or even thousands of dollars back into your pocket with minimal effort and stress, and from now on bills will fear you, your family will thank you, and friends will love you for the tips you can give them on surviving the cost of living crisis.

And you've earned one last side-splitting dad joke too: Two oranges walk into a bar. One says to the other, 'You're round.'

Go forth and enjoy your windfalls and winnings, and thank you for reading.

MONEY-SAVING WEBSITES & APPS

OneBigSwitch.com.au – This is where I work. We use the People Power of over one million Australians who have joined up since 2011 to negotiate group discounts on household bills and source the best money-saving info. It's free to join. Get on board.

OzBargain.com.au – Australia's #1 online community for hardcore hunters of 'deals, vouchers, coupons, discounts and freebies'. Community members post everything from home loan deals they've spotted to discounts on KFC, then the deals get ranked according to how many like them. I thought I was into money-saving until I visited this site but their dedication to killing bills is on a whole different level!

EnergyMadeEasy.gov.au – The government website for comparing electricity and gas deals across NSW, South-east Qld, the ACT, Tasmania and SA. It's very good and even allows you to upload a recent PDF email bill rather than manually typing in all your info. Frustratingly, it does not include how each plan compares to the Government Reference Price, because it gives you a real estimate based on your particular usage. But it does rank your options from cheapest to most expensive and more people should use this website as a starting point for saving on power bills.

Compare.energy.vic.gov.au – The government website for comparing electricity and gas deals across Victoria. Same as above - it's also very good, except for a few pieces of missing information.

Wattever.com.au – The most comprehensive commercial energy comparison website in Australia, because it attempts to include ALL publicly-available plans and not just those that it's paid to promote. Wattever also says it will not call you once you've got a quote, unlike other commercial comparison sites.

Canstar.com.au – Australia's 'biggest' (i.e. most comprehensive) comparison site, with over 800 brands compared. They also have a system of awards and star ratings that help you work out which brands are the real deal and which ones are pretenders.

Finder.com.au – Australia's 'most-visited' comparison site. Started with credit cards and has branched out to cover multiple products. These guys specialise in content to maximise their Google search results: they've got articles on just about any question you could want answered on money and personal finance. They're also pioneers in the 'money-saving app' area, and they're obsessed with cryptocurrency.

CompareClub.com.au - the 4th of the 'Big Four' comparison sites in Australia, and possibly the fastest-growing out of the lot. They also work with cashback websites, so you can get, for example, up to $70 cashback if you use their energy switching service.

Comparethemarket.com.au – One of the biggest commercial comparison websites in Australia, they built their business by helping people save on health insurance and car insurance but now they cover everything from energy plans to travel insurance too. They don't compare all providers, but they really know their stuff, and it's a free service. They now own iSelect too.

PrivateHealth.gov.au – The government website for comparing all the health insurance deals available across Australia. It's comprehensive but it's clunky so unless you're determined to do it all yourself, use one of the commercial sites below.

ACCC.gov.au – The competition and consumer watchdog's website has all sorts of useful info, particularly on their pet topics of petrol, the NBN and online shopping. They've also got extensive information on your consumer rights, from how to complain, to warranties, product safety and scams!

Moneysmart.gov.au – This is the corporate regulator ASIC's consumer info website, and it's chock-a-block full of information on everything from insurance to banking, credit and super. But the best reason to visit is the dozens of tools: mortgage switching calculators, credit card calculators, retirement calculators, and apps to help you buy a car, track your spend or cultivate good saving habits.

FinancialRights.gov.au - The Financial Rights Legal Centre offers free advice and advocacy for consumers who are in financial stress. There are sample letters, fact sheets, a National Debt Helpline and a tool to use if you're in a car crash and you need to work out what to do next.

AFCA.org.au – The Australian Financial Complaints Authority is a newish super-ombudsman for credit, banking, insurance, investments and superannuation complaints. If you've tried to get a resolution from your provider and had no luck, this is the place to go next.

Ombudsman.gov.au – The Commonwealth Ombudsman deals with a range of complaints and health insurance is one of their areas. They publish a bunch of fact sheets and brochures, they run the government comparison website and they have an independent complaint-handling service.

TIO.com.au – TIO is your new best friend if you've tried and failed to get a problem with your telco fixed. The Telecommunications Industry Ombudsman is industry-funded but independently governed, and it can make enforceable decisions about complaints up to $50,000, and make recommendations up to $100,000.

Your local Energy Ombudsman – This is where to go if you have a dispute with your power company and you haven't been able to get a resolution by contacting the provider first.

- NSW Energy & Water Ombudsman:
  www.ewon.com.au
- Energy & Water Ombudsman Victoria:
  www.ewov.com.au
- Energy & Water Ombudsman Queensland:
  www.ewoq.com.au
- Energy & Water Ombudsman SA:
  www.ewosa.com.au
- Energy & Water Ombudsman WA:
  www.ombudsman.wa.gov.au/energyandwater
- Energy Ombudsman Tasmania:
  www.energyombudsman.tas.gov.au
- Energy Ombudsman ACT:
  www.acat.act.gov.au

ABOUT THE AUTHOR

I live in south-east Sydney near the beach with my wife, two kids and Sunny the Money-Saving Dog.

I love saving people money – it's the biggest kick I get from my job.

I never thought I'd end up doing this for a living. In a former life I got 100 in my HSC, wrote jokes for *The Chaser* newspaper, had a monthly wine column in a glossy magazine, studied three-fifths of a law degree and worked at *The Sydney Morning Herald* for ten years, interviewing celebrities, pollies, crooks (and sometimes people who were all of the above).

I probably knew less than you do about saving money and everything about spending it – and I *never* talked about household bills at barbecues.

But then I started working at One Big Switch because I was excited by the idea of group switching, which uses the combined

People Power of a million-plus member households to negotiate cheaper prices on household bills.

I learnt about money-saving on the job and it became my passion. So from there I ended up back in the media as a Money columnist at *The Sydney Morning Herald* and *The Age*, and the *Today* show, 2GB, 4BC and ABC Radio as a regular talking head.

I've also been a brand ambassador or spokesman for providers including amaysim, Tangerine, Cashrewards and Remediator – because I like working with businesses that are genuine about saving people money.

Over the past decade, I've learnt most of what there is to know about how to save a buck – or thousands of bucks – on your bills, as easily as possible.

Hopefully by now you've learnt a lot of it too, simply by reading this book. If you have, do me a favour and tell someone. Lend them your book, buy them their own, or just crow about your money-saving brilliance on social media and tag me.

Because these tricks, hacks and loopholes have maybe never been more important to know and every time someone celebrates a win in the war on bills, they inspire someone else to have a go.